Walking Ollie

Walking Ollie

STEPHEN FOSTER

✳ SHORT BOOKS

First published in 2006 by
Short Books
3A Exmouth House
Pine Street
London EC1R 0JH

This paperback edition published in 2007
10 9 8 7 6

A CIP catalogue record for this book
is available from the British Library.

ISBN 978-1-904977-88-9

Printed in the UK by CPI Bookmarque, Croydon, CR0 4TD
a member of the CPI group of companies

For T.A.

*It was in the winter of 2003 that I became a dog owner.
Though I had heard that animal psychologists exist, and
no doubt thrive, on the West Coast of the United States
and in Manhattan, I was not aware that they had arrived
here, much less had I ever considered the idea that the
holder of such a position would come to visit my
home more than once.*

PREFACE

It's an October evening, night is falling, it's getting cold, colder than I'm dressed for, and I'm heading across parkland in the opposite direction to the way I intended to go.

I continue in the wrong direction in the company of a stranger, and in the knowledge that by the time I get home I'll have missed the kick-off of a televised football match that I mean to watch. The detour comes about because the stranger has a dog with him – a young whippet – and Ollie, the hero of this book, has introduced himself to the whippet by shooting off after her (against my instructions), and surprising her from behind. As I catch up the pair of them are circling and sniffing at each other's private parts like nobody's business.

Ollie is at an advantage because the whippet is on a lead. She is on the lead because she and her owner are walking on a road which divides the parkland. There's no traffic nearby, or even in the distance: it's quiet enough that I can *hear* that this is the case. But still: it *is* a road. I halt Ollie in his circling and sniffing by putting him on his lead too, explaining to the man that I am vexed with the dog because some time ago he was knocked over, and I would prefer for this not to happen to him again. I do not shout at Ollie for his disobedience, though, or otherwise tell him off, because this only freaks him out. I just give him a stern look. The owner of the whippet takes an interest in the tale of the accident. It is, after all, a cautionary tale.

'Is he okay now then?' he asks.

'Yes, more or less,' I say. 'He broke his leg, but that seems to be completely fixed (touch wood). It's just the mental side that continues to give grief.'

I could tap my finger to my temple here, to indicate that Ollie is a bit round the bend. He seems to learn nothing from experience. He would run into a car as soon as blink, though he will always jump out of harm's way if a fearsome carrier bag blows by. A carrier bag has never hurt him, a car has put him into hospital. Nothing of this registers with Ollie, he makes no connection between cause and effect.

By now, I am used to it, used to his ways, can anticipate some of them, and even find them endearing (which is why I *don't* tap my finger to my temple), though at moments like this, when he disobeys me in a way that could get him killed, I suck in air and swear under my breath.

The whippet owner looks at Ollie. 'His coat is very shiny,' he says.

'Yes,' I reply, 'I think it's down to fish oil – he's very partial to pilchards.'

'Pilchards?' he says.

'Yes.' I reply. 'In tomato sauce.'

'Would they play, if we let them off?' the whippet owner asks. He glances at Ollie once more. It's clear from Ollie's general attitude that this is a suggestion that he rates very highly. The owner looks at me. The look is a further question, one which says all of the following: it would be nice for them to have a run, but a lot of dog walkers I meet are reluctant for this to happen; is it because my dog is a whippet, because she is fast — or what?

It might be because of her breed and speed, but it is more likely to be 'or what'. Dog owners are weird, curious people, full of 'or whats'. All people are weird and curious, I know that, but dog owners are top of the range in this respect. This is the conclusion I have arrived at since I joined their cult (and, as a consequence of joining, I have become a weirder and curiouser person too).

Whether I care to admit it or not, I am now like them, spending much of my time absorbed and obsessed by the goings on in my pet's life. I am to be found outdoors in all manner of foul weathers, walking in the opposite direction to the one which I intended, entirely for Ollie's benefit. The reason, to answer the young whippet owner's question, that some owners won't let their dogs play, are plentiful and complex — because they are miserable sods, because they are fay, because their animal runs off and won't come back, because they are filled with a proxy neurosis on Fido's behalf: they don't want the dog getting hurt, injured, lost, or bullied. I prefer this not to happen to my dog either, but the urge that Ollie needs to satisfy more than any other in his life is the freedom to let rip, so I see that he gets it, whatever the cost to me in terms of missed kick-offs, lost time, and walking in the wrong direction.

I offer the benefit of my observations on why some won't let their dogs play as I walk along with the whippet owner. His dog is only six months old; Ollie is about four years now: I am experienced at this game, a veteran.

'Follow me,' I say. 'Round here through this copse of trees – just behind there's a field where they can have a proper run.'

Let loose, the pair of them perform loops round an imaginary greyhound track, using each other as the hare; finally they pause to catch breath, and while they rest they chew each other's ears and play-fight until they appear to be beat; and then they do it all again, over-and-over, until they have run themselves into the ground and can barely stand. I find all this a thing of beauty, an aesthetic delight, a visceral therapy. I can watch it for a long time.

When they are exhausted and all that's left of them are their vapours, the whippet owner goes on his way, and Ollie and I head off across the dark fields, back towards my car. As we do so, another dog emerges from nowhere, a bouncing Labrador, and Ollie, finding his seventh second wind, starts the chase all over again. A girl appears out of the gloom, shouting at the Labrador and apologising for the interruption.

'He's always running off,' she says.

'It's okay,' I say, 'Ollie was like that, when he was young.' (This last is a lie, one of the stories I tell; he still behaves in this way, of course, and often enough – we have seen it once already and we're only in the preface.)

'How long did it go on for?' she asks.

I know this question, from other encounters, and I understand that it doubles as a probe for further enlightenment; might I be able to advise her when, exactly, the bad behaviour in her *own* pet will cease? Will this naughty Labrador ever become well-behaved, like Ollie?

'How old is yours?' I ask.

'Nine months,' she replies.

They are the second young-dog-and-new-owner combination in a row. I make a short statement as if I know what I'm talking about, offering reassurance with all the authority of a provincial solicitor.

'It took Ollie about a year to get there, so probably not long for you to go now. It's just the exuberance of youth, you know, they're like badly behaved kids for a while, it's totally natural. I'm sure yours will settle down soon.'

'Oh,' she says, 'Good, there's hope for us yet.'

As I come out with my patter Ollie starts to mount the Labrador, apparently having sex with it from behind (Labradors are to Ollie what French women are to some men – a breed that unfailingly arouse his amour). She looks at Ollie and his erotic intent towards her dog (who is also male), and she looks back to me, for my explanation. After all, I seem to know what I'm talking about.

'It's just a dominance game, that,' I say dismissively, 'It doesn't mean a thing.'

'Right,' she says.

***

Ollie was nearer to two years old before he was anything like 'settled down', and he still turns the deaf ear whenever he sights a matter in the distance that requires his urgent attention – like a whippet on the road ahead. He always looks back to check before he sets off, so that I can tell him 'No!' and he can safely ignore my command. I mention nothing of this to the Labrador owner as we take our leave. But Ollie decides to follow me at heel, as it happens, suddenly pretending to be the well-trained animal I make him out to be.

It's our first dark walk of the approaching winter. Ollie trots alongside and slightly ahead, like a gymkhana horse, keeping close, as though he's looking out for me, as though he knows that humans are retarded when it comes to night-vision, as though he's actually performing the role of guide, being a help. It's not like him, and yet, a little bit, it *is* like him too. We have our moments when we are man and dog, at one with each other, and at one with that other weird and curious thing: nature. But it has not always been this way, nowhere near.

Ollie is a rescue dog. Worse than that, he is a rescue *lurcher*, and worse than that he is a rescue lurcher with *Saluki* in him. If this last is meaningless to you, not to worry; it was meaningless to me too, when, one snowy winter afternoon, Ollie was introduced to us: a deceptively cheerful sliver of pup looking for somewhere to call home.

THE LURCHER BREEDER

A lurcher is defined as follows: half-greyhound, half something else. The something else is most frequently a collie-type scruffy-coated dog, so the classic lurcher look inclines to the great unwashed. Lurchers are grunge. If you pause to notice you'll see that they are the typical companions of street dwellers, who will often have one curled up next to the begging bowl. This tells you something about street dwellers – lurchers tend to take at least as much from their surroundings in the way of heat as they give out. But then they do have a specific talent which will be helpful if you are hungry and homeless: they are the poacher's dog of choice. The combined speeding instinct of the greyhound coupled with the intelligent herding gene of the collie scruff produces a very fast animal that is agile, sharp, and expert at quick turns, and so is ideally suited to sighting and picking up rabbits. They are often bred by itinerants for the activities of hare-coursing and baiting, and for lamping (chasing rabbits and game at night, using lamplight.)

Beside the more common collie-type, there are other many other lurcher matings; Ollie's non-greyhound side is Saluki. The pure Saluki, I discover, is of Arabic origin, by all accounts notoriously aloof, stand-offish and superior. The Saluki-greyhound, as it turns out, is a particularly specialised and perverse version of a lurcher.

But not only had I never heard of a Saluki when we picked Ollie up, neither did I know he had such a side; at that point he was just the aforementioned sliver of pup.

***

About a year after Ollie had arrived, I found myself being driven from Knock Airport in County Mayo down to Galway City, a taxi ride lasting the better part of two hours.

The driver, a stocky man called Shay, was a comic. As he took our bags, he warmed up with a spiel about the use of the word 'International' on the airport exterior, developed a routine centred on the quality of the coffee available to the waiting cabbie inside the terminal building, and hit his stride as he gave his opinion on the newly established ban on smoking in public environments that some idiots had introduced – in Ireland of all the feckin' places – a law which meant he'd had to leave the International Airport building in order to drink the cup of anaemic piss while he lit a fag as he awaited the late arrival of our flight.

Before we left the International Airport carpark – where parking prices were absurd, a pure joke – Shay mentioned that his own place of work, as it happened, was an exemption to the laughable new smoking law, if that was okay. As he drove and smoked, he told lurid tales about the night girls of Galway City and other associated matters; Knock airport might not be so

'International', for instance, but it was this very aspect that made it such a convenient hub for the trading of narcotics.

As if to prove his point, two Garda roadblocks had been set up, at each of which it was established that there were no drug mules travelling in his car. Neither of these encounters with the coppers had any effect on Shay's flouting of the smoking law.

As we moved south and the scenery became more verdant, I spotted some horses in a field. Shay had quit the drinking, and also, it emerged, the gambling, so the talk about the horses was brief and bitter but it led on to a conversation about dogs. This was happier territory. Shay told me that he was a lurcher breeder.

'Oh,' I said, 'I've got one of those.'

'What cross?' he asked, the insider's question. When I said Saluki-greyhound, he rolled his enormous eyes, snorted, and began to tell me how he'd once been good enough to offer such an animal an opportunity to prove itself, but that the damn thing was so hopeless, troublesome and unsatisfactory in so many different ways that, after giving it more last chances than it deserved, he had been forced to take it down to the garden and shoot it.

About a year earlier I may have regarded this as a callous act of brutality; in the light of my recent experiences I could see his point only too well.

'What do you do with yours, then?' he asked, meaning, I imagined, was there any slight chance that Ollie was remotely adept at picking up rabbits and coursing for hares?

'Well,' I said, 'Mostly he sits on his sofa in his sleeping bag, while I tickle him behind his ears and tell him that he's a good boy.'

Shay was delighted with this. He laughed long and hard at the amateur concept of wasting your time by introducing fairy-tale ideas into the mind of a creature who deserves nothing better than what he's got coming to him. As we parted company Shay gave me his number. One day I'm to phone him and he'll teach me how to train a lurcher properly, in order that it can be useful and earn its keep. And one day I really do intend to make that call.

In the meantime:

MINGUS

The idea of acquiring a dog at all began with Mingus. Mingus is a Dalmatian. He is the former pet of my partner, Trezza. Mingus lives in Derby with Trezza's ex, but he comes to stop with us in Norwich sometimes for the occasional custody visit. In the days and weeks after Mingus has left to return to his Master you will find Trezza in melancholy mood.

Mingus is the first dog I've ever had in my home. He is nice to look at, but it's more or less downhill from there. Here is an animal who will eat anything, who will display interest in any item that could possibly be comestible, with the sole exception of oranges. Drool falls in thick spools from his jowls as he sits in the kitchen keeping me under surveillance whenever I'm cooking, whatever I'm cooking, whatever I'm assembling; he does not even rule out Cornflakes. I find it hard work to conceal my distaste at the drool, though I try, for his sake. He has a deep soulful look and I don't want to offend him, I do not want to precipitate the sadness that comes so quickly to a dog's eyes by having him notice that I'm disgusted by a habit that he cannot help.

He has other habits I could live without too, like coming up to our bedroom at five in the morning to check we are still alive by licking our faces. It's considerate of him, but it's a kindness I would pass on, were it possible. We could close the bedroom door, but he would just scratch his way through it; persistence is one of his main characteristics.

His surprisingly sharp and tenacious white hairs, which attach themselves to any fabric and to every other surface as well, are dismaying. For me, it would be better if his spots moulted instead as a good part of my wardrobe, about which I am touchy, is in the dark-to-black end of the colour spectrum. Prior to

Mingus's visits I hide my regular clothes away, and for the duration of his stay I wear items that I normally reserve for decorating. I am touchy about the interior cleanliness of my car, too. So when we make a journey with Mingus I pre-drape the rear seats and headrests using the dust sheets that go with the decorating outfit. This protects against the drool, which is chemical in its power to decompose upholstery, but as for the hairs – which multiply faster than frogspawn and generate enough static to light a Christmas tree – there's nothing to be done. I am still finding them months later.

I could easily get by without any of this, and most of the time, of course, I do.

But.

(But is often a doleful conjunctive, but not in this case, where it is active and crucial):

But I am fond of Mingus. It is not actually all downhill. He is a charming and endearing presence. When you walk with him you find that family groups will approach you expectantly and you are able to say, in a proprietorial manner, 'Yes he is very friendly – go ahead, stroke him if you like.' And so they do, and he takes it in his stride. Mingus is a natural celebrity who recognises his obligation to his public, and who deals with it professionally. He goes for the regal approach – his equivalent of Her Majesty's restrained wave is the half-nod of acknowledgement, delivered with a self-assurance that derives from being so well-bred and so handsome. It goes without saying that his public reception has a great deal to do with the received image and status that his breed enjoys as a consequence of the 101 Dalmatians books and films, which, as you'd expect from cartoon fantasies, are not big on the downside of doggyness. But still, as I watch him being stroked, and I see the happiness it brings, it's easy to forget about the drool, and the hairs, and the other matters – most specifically the crap – and at these moments I pretend to be Mingus's real owner.

It's during Mingus's first stay over, while walking out in the pouring rain for the fourth time in two days, that the principal life-changing aspect of caring for a dog really comes home: a dog demands a frequent workout. If a proper dog (goodbye dear Chihuahua owner, but I fear this is not the book for you) does not exert itself twice daily, it will become an unseemly tub of tripe. A tour round the block will not do. The animal needs a run – ergo the single most alarming aspect of dog ownership: you are forced into direct contact with nature.

For myself, even without a dog, I take my exercise. I am forty-odd, and have reached a typical forty-odd condition whereby the endorphin-kick of aerobic exertion has almost eclipsed my addiction to nicotine. But of course I do not *walk* to the gym, squash court, five-a-side pitch or swimming pool. Exercise is its own end, it is not for getting from A to B. That is why I have a nice car.

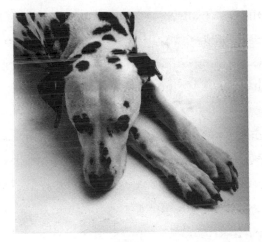

Mingus

Mingus visits are, then, the only times I find myself with my feet on the actual ground, walking (anaerobic, worthless, endorphin-kick-free exercise) in those messy woodlands, commons and meadows (without a dog I can see no reason why a human should ever need to be in a meadow) with which I would normally have no acquaintance. These areas are simply the green backgrounds that I fail to notice through the window of the nice car as I drive past them. Though I sometimes jog around a sports field, a sports field is too cultivated and flat and tidy to fit the description 'nature'. Nature has long grass, is unstructured, often slippery underfoot, and has insects and small animals living in it; it's an environment about which I could not care less: verdant, necessary to life and so on, but about as thrilling as a Methodist sermon.

I was sent to Methodist church when I was a young boy growing up in the soot-coated city of Stoke-on-Trent. Not because we are religious, but because that was where your parents sent you on a Sunday so that they could have some peace and quiet. After the thrilling sermon there was the thrilling Sunday School lesson. Occasionally, Sunday School trips to the countryside were organised in order that we might take fresh air, cleanse our souls, and learn to identify flora and fauna by name. I would hang at the back of these excursions in a cloud, wishing I was a Catholic. I had no interest in being able to identify flora and fauna by name and this has never changed; my inner Christian scholar is more than satisfied by knowing a great deal more about football than is necessary, and by attempting to interpret information regarding the form of horses.

But as a consequence of having Mingus around, by liking being with him, by hosting him as he spread his largesse into the world, I began to discover that, when it came down to it, I didn't actively mind, all that much, walking in nature. I remain immune to specific knowledge of bird variety, but I like their songs. As the trees change in time with the seasons, I'm struck by the shifting sculpture of the landscape. When the sun comes out after the rain, I like the smell. In the right mood I even like the rain itself. In short, it's not as bad as I remembered it.

There is something I mind, though, and I mind it a lot. It is the inescapable, extra awful aspect of Mingus and every other member of his species: he, and they, will shamelessly relieve their bowls wherever they like. I despise dealing with turds. Crouching to 'pick-up' is not a job for a man. It is fresh turd, too, remember, it is at its most stinking. And you can count yourself lucky if it's a fresh stinking log or three, which is at least manageable, and not a fresh stinking pile, which isn't. You sheath yourself from excrement-direct-to-flesh contact only by the gauge of a plastic bag as you lean forward to gather the stuff, while simultaneously and instinctively leaning back, away from the stench. You could not patent a more perfect method for putting your back out; here is the reason why many a dog owner walks with a stoop.

You *could* use a pooper scooper of course, which would give you the benefit of a little distance, but after using it you would be carrying a shitty spade about. For me this is a significant design flaw. They could invent a disposable pooper scooper, I suppose, but as you are already holding a bagged-up turd for which you can find no bin, where would you get rid of the disposable pooper scooper?

As a matter of nasal self-preservation you develop tactics to avoid picking up. A 'Do Nots' list accumulates in your mind. Do not walk him on a pavement with a narrow greensward alongside it that he will only regard as a crapoir. Do not take him across the road at the traffic lights, so he can demonstrate his dumping skills to motorists stopped on red. Do not tie him up outside a newsagent's. Do not take a short cut through a supermarket carpark. Do not take him to a Piazza, a square, or a shopping mall. *Never* walk him through a town centre.

Instead, encourage him to poo in the garden before he leaves the house. Pointless, he will refuse to do that as it would be unhygienic to go to the toilet in his own personal space. He will regard you curiously, wondering how he has managed to get himself involved with a human as dim as you are. The expression on his face will say, 'No, not *here*; how many times do we have to go through this?'

If you are going to become a long-term dog person, here is the way to deal with defecation: first thing in the morning launch the animal into the back of the car (trade in the nice sports coupé while it's still got some residual value, it's a battered estate you're looking for). Drive the battered estate to a copse – an especially overgrown part of nature: a meadow with trees and bushes. Park as near to the copse as possible and let him directly into it.

Using this method, his bottom's first prolonged contact with the chilly air that unfailingly provokes the turd (unless he's in his own garden, of course), will take place in an area where you can leave it behind. This may represent a violation of a by-law, but there is fox, rabbit, vole and mouse shit in there as well, so, like the foxes, rabbits, voles and mice that went before him, you can feel free to abandon the evil item. Like a person who has just silently farted, you can move along on your way with a more or less clear conscience.

Meanwhile, what remains behind can be assumed to provide a fertile, manure-type base in which further examples of nature can flourish. In this manner, instead of engaging yourself in odious and demeaning pooper-scooper activity, you have instead become part of a virtuous life-cycle. After the poo(s) (there may be more than one) and the lovely walk in nature, back home in the warm kitchen, Mingus will look at you adoringly with his head tipped to one side. This is because you are holding a pork pie. For the price of half of it he will love you. For the price of the other half he will protect you from attack and lay down his life in defence of yours.

It was through knowing, and liking, Mingus that I was able to begin to think of myself as a person who might have a part-share in a dog.

And so it was, on the snowy winter afternoon, that I found myself at a re-homing kennels considering the idea that a pair of Deerhounds the size of donkeys might come to live in our house.

ERNIE

We make the journey to the National Canine Defence League (NCDL) dogs' home at Snetterton, in Norfolk, with the intention of looking for a retired greyhound. Helping a sporting refugee would be an act of kindness that would also provide Trezza with the opportunity to enjoy a little light walk everyday. Her sedentary occupation as a writer, and her disdain for the gymnasium and new-fangled faddish ideas of the like, means she doesn't take much exercise. Moreover, a dog of our own will help her to cope with the melancholies that Mingus's departures herald. It is *me* who suggests this. In a sense, the whole dog project is mine.

There are false starts on the road to Snetterton. We begin by conducting idle conversations about what sort of dog we'd have, if we were to have one. First off, we would not consider a Dalmatian as any other Dalmatian would not be Mingus. Next, we eliminate certain other breeds for being too small, or too big, or too hairy, or too stupid, or too stupid-looking (which is often the same thing), or just the kind of dog we don't like for no good reason we can explain.

While queuing for a coffee in a concession within a DIY Superstore one morning, I notice a pile of books in an aisle. The book pile is that of a coffee-table title called *The Giant Book of the Dog*. I browse *The Giant Book of the Dog* over a cappuccino. It looks as though it could be helpful, and at £4.99 it's a bargain. At night-time, in bed, I study the pages at length. I come to the conclusion that what we need is a Hungarian Vizsla. The Vizsla is short-haired, slightly taller than average, well-proportioned, and purposeful-looking with a noble bearing and silky ears. If it were a horse the Vizsla's colour would be described as a chestnut. To me this animal seems to epitomise the essence of what a dog should be.

Additionally, the notes state that the Vizsla makes a first-class pet and is good with children. Not that we regularly have children about the place, but you're bound to come across them while you're out. Whether or not *The Giant Book of the Dog* is to be entirely trusted in its assessment of breed character/child suitability is a moot point, however, as in my lengthy study I note that there are very few breeds which are not first class pets who are good with children.

The Hungarian Vizsla is a gundog, developed by Magyar noblemen to pick up game and geese and ducks and so on. We have no need for this in our lives. But then Britain's most popular breed, the Labrador, or Labrador Retriever (soon, for a time, to become my least favourite), is listed under the same category. These classifications are surely meaningless, I think, when it's a pet you're looking for: like the people who carry the Labrador to the DIY Superstore in the four-wheel SUV, the animal within is no more likely to be put to its use than the bull-bars welded to the front of their vehicle.

This could be why so many Labrador retrievers are

fatter than their irritating owners, but this is a subject for ranting about later, once I have an animal of my own, when I have experience, when I have formed views. Back then, lying in bed looking at the pictures of all the child-friendly dogs, I knew nothing, and it was in this happy state that we visited a specialist Vizsla lady whose bitch was carrying a litter.

The lady lived near Reading, a hundred and seventy miles away. I found her through the Vizsla Society who have a website, as do practically all breeds. I phoned the Society, and was put through to the Puppy Secretary who advised that the Reading specialist had a litter on the way. Good news, but first of all I put my most pressing concern to the Puppy Secretary: I asked if Vizslas were nice to stroke; I had read on the website that their coat was 'oily' and I did not like the idea of this.

'Think of velvet,' she said, 'it's rather like that.' Velvetiness sounded altogether different, a huge improvement on oiliness, and set my mind at rest concerning the matter of coat-feel. I could tell by the her tone, though, that the question I'd asked gave the game away just as effectively as commenting on the colour of a second-hand car does if you're a female buyer.

Reading in Berkshire is not near to Norwich in Norfolk, but we could at least tie-in a viewing (of the mother, not the puppy itself, which was not yet born, this was how the matter was to proceed) with a football match or a race meeting.

We arrived at the Vizsla lady's house and met her two Vizslas – the pregnant mother, and the grandmother-in-waiting. I already knew a good deal about these animals because the telephone call to arrange the visit had lasted for over an hour. The dogs were bouncy and enthusiastic in their welcome: I don't like being licked on the face, I find it a bit much coming from a creature which, though it won't go to the toilet in its own garden, will do more or less anything else that is unspeakable.

The expression 'the dog's bollocks', for example, is entirely obvious in its origination, and as I came to spend more time in their company, I noted that dogs rule out absolutely nothing (with the exception of oranges) in terms of what they might put in their mouths – the first time I saw Ollie nibbling at a pile of horse manure I was appalled, though not as much as when I first caught him trying out his own vomit as a between-meals snack.

My initial impression was that the Vizslas didn't look all that much like the picture in *The Giant Book of the Dog*. To begin with, they were smaller and slighter. This was because they were bitches, not dogs. I had read about this difference regarding size-relative-to-gender, determined by the highest point at withers (shoulders), but I had not seen it in real life until now; in fact, this was the first time I'd seen a Vizsla in real life at all. They were a different shade to the picture too, more dun. I looked at them like I would look at a rare animal in a zoo; I found them fascinating, and beautiful, and slightly unnerving all at once, and equally out of keeping with their environment. They lived in a very tidy, small modern house in a cul-de-sac.

After we had made friends with 'the girls' (we were given treats to feed to them), we all went out for a walk in nearby woods, a walk which lasted for a good hour and a half. This struck me as pretty stiff, not to mention a huge amount of time to be blowing on anaerobic exercise.

During the walk we were quizzed about our home, our surroundings, our backgrounds and our lifestyle. Trezza is a regular smoker, but I knew for certain she would not be mentioning this, nor lighting up, during the critical period of scrutiny. The Vizsla lady was interviewing us to see that we were fit people to own a dog from her lineage; it went without saying that an environment that endorsed passive smoking would be unsuitable. Occasional asides were made about the girls themselves who disappeared in and out of the bushes and trees, though never too far out of sight. They were well behaved, if not a little reserved. They cantered very stylishly as each had an excellent 'hip-score'. I considered pretending that I knew what this meant, but curiosity got the better of me.

Hip-scoring is to do with the way in which the ball joints at the top of the hind legs sit in the pelvic girdle, and the knock-on effect this has on leg-alignment and associated matters. Vets can issue hip-score ratings according to how much fractional deviation the hind legs display compared against an ideal norm. A low hip-score is the one to have if you intend to show your dog; otherwise it's of little consequence unless it's so far out that the dog is bandy, but I guess you'd notice that yourself without the need for the hip-score.

While I was learning about this I picked up a stick, a broken branch, which I made to throw for these girls with great hips. Out of the corner of my eye I saw the lady freeze.

'Do they chase sticks?' I asked, arm cocked, stick unthrown.

'It can be a little dangerous,' she replied, 'If they catch them in their throats, you know, they could choke, or do untold other damage.'

We walked on, and, when the girls were not looking, I quietly abandoned the hazard. Although I hadn't actually hurled it – and imagine if my aim had been off – I wondered how badly the suggestion would count against us. The lady helped ease the atmosphere by saying a ball might be all right, in a nice big field, or similar. I mentioned that Norwich was near to the coast, which would be lovely for walking and for throwing a ball for a puppy to fetch. This sounded good. I remembered that we both work from home so the little animal would have company all day long. This sounded good, too. I watched the girls closely now. I was much taken with the way they moved in and out of the trees; they were athletes. Their owner began making various toots on her whistle to which the girls did, or sometimes did not, respond, according to whether or not they had a scent, but their behaviour was generally exemplary – at the end of their walk they stopped well short of the road to have their leads put on, and over in the carpark they made graceful jumps into the back of the car.

Returning to the house, we watched as the Vizsla lady washed and dried the dog's paws and 'little bellies' in a bucket outside the front door, before they were allowed back inside. I glanced around hoping nobody would see me taking part in this activity, and in so doing I glanced at Trezza. Trezza had visited dog breeders before, when she was finding Mingus. My glance said, 'This isn't normal, surely?' Her return glance confirmed that it wasn't.

In the kitchen the girls were fed individual diets of hypo-allergenic food; I was unsurprised to learn that, even given this diet, one of them was a faddy eater. We had not been into the kitchen before the walk. The walls were obliterated by rosettes, medallions and cer-tificates, which the girls had won at shows all over the country.

Crufts was mentioned. A Vizsla notepad on the fridge was secured by a Vizsla fridge magnet. I should know better, because, at a price, anything is available in the world, but I was astonished that such accessories existed. I studied a certificate. It was for first prize. I studied another certificate. That was for first prize, too. I hadn't realised that we'd been walking with aristocrats — I thought they were just pedigree. It appeared that this pair were even posher than Mingus.

'Tea?' said the lady. While the kettle was boiling, she talked to the girls and explained their differing characteristics and special ways to *them* for *our* benefit, a history which was interspersed with some bitter asides concerning her ex-partner.

Together with our tray of drinks and the biscuit tin, we rejoined the animals who had heard enough about themselves and had withdrawn to curl up in their separate baskets in the lounge. I fed one of them a piece of digestive before I'd had time to think better of it but the lady didn't seem to mind, she was more relaxed now she had taken her exercise and her girls were safely back home unharmed with clean paws and bellies, and that the visitors seemed to approve of the family. Finally, after a further half-hour of Vizsla stories, we excused ourselves from the viewing.

We had arrived nearly four hours earlier, not long after lunch. It was now officially time for a drink. But first things first. We drove round the corner and I stopped the car so that Trezza could get out and have a fag, and I even had one myself. As I rolled it I conjured a picture of the lady's ex, and considered how difficult it must have been for him to compete with the girls. Would that be my fate if we went through with this? Hopefully not, because there was a specific question that I needed to raise right away:

'That woman was mad, wasn't she?' I said.

Trezza nodded and carried on inhaling.

'Are all dog breeders like that?'

'A little bit, yes,' she replied. 'But she was...' Trezza exhaled enormously while searching for the *mot juste* '...she was *unique*.'

'What d'you think of the dogs, though?' I said. They'd seemed pretty nice to me.

'Lovely,' said Trezza, 'Very sweet. Quite normal, considering.'

Following the viewing we stopped over at Fawlty Towers, Reading, in order that we could watch Stoke City the next day. Stoke played one of Icelandic manager Gudjon Thordarson's late-period 5-3-2 away formation experiments – a system that might well have been devised by Manuel – and lost the match, throwing away their last slim chance of automatic promotion in the process. A sorry situation, but one I was well used to.

Back in Norwich we phoned the lady and said that, if it was all right with her, we'd really like a puppy. She assured us that we were top of the list of suitable parents. We broke out the champagne. The price agreed was six hundred pounds.

Though we were invited back for ongoing viewings of the bitch during her pregnancy, we considered this above and beyond the call of duty, and, as it turned out, we never did acquire an animal from this source because the mother delivered only one pup in a difficult Caesarean operation. Her owner could not bear the thought of it living as far afield as Norfolk, and I think we understood.

There was a further false start involving a visit to a Vizsla breeder in the South Downs. This woman was also idiosyncratic in that she had fourteen dogs of her own which carpeted her kitchen wall-to-wall. Half were Vizslas and half were Labradors. She impressed me by addressing them all individually when, to my untrained eye, each set of seven looked very much alike. She had a litter of eight for us to see, and if we didn't fancy any of *them* there was another lot coming along straight after that from another of the thirteen bitches in the kitchen. The pups we were taken to look at were kept in a special whelping shed in the grounds of the farmhouse. They were a few weeks old, and for the same six hundred (Vizsla price-fixing appeared to be organised by an effective cartel) we could take our pick and collect in a few weeks' time. We selected a dog, the one that had the nicest ears and the most in the way of personality, we admired all the certificates and rosettes on the kitchen wall, and, as we took our leave, the next client exchanged parking spaces with us. She was a young woman driving a new Porsche.

The word 'Wiemaraner' had come up in the breeder's kitchen. Wiemaraners are those rather beautiful soft grey dogs that are fetishised by the art photographer William Wegman, and often appear in television adverts. They became a yuppie accessory in the Nineties and something of that image has stuck (I have yet to meet a Wiemaraner owner who has managed to lower themselves far enough to speak to me). The arrival of the young woman in the new Porsche made me wonder whether Vizslas might be about to become the new Wiemaraners. Still, that wouldn't be my problem, because I live in Norfolk where owning a gundog is an obvious and natural thing to do, not in South Kensington, where it isn't.

On the drive back from Sussex, I began to do sums in my head along the lines of eight times 600 equals roughly five grand a litter, five grand times 14 dogs equals £70,000 even if they're only in season once a year – when in fact they're in season twice a year – so, if all goes well, you can call that £140,000 per annum, gross. Like most writers, I waste a huge amount of mental energy considering more profitable ways of spending my life.

In the middle of this mental arithmetic, an argument began in my left ear concerning the overloading of my time-table. I had sprung the visit to the breeder on Trezza as a surprise bonus after some activity we'd been doing in the capital, for which I had also given inadequate warning.

Suddenly, from nowhere, I found myself on the receiving end of an extended lecture about how I had no time for puppy training and all the rest that went with it, did I, and that the poor dog would never be out of the kennels, would it, or was the plan that *she* looked after it while I continued with my lifestyle regardless – football matches, games of squash, race meetings and so on – not to say all the activities I'd arranged without any consultation and then forgotten to mention. We concluded the discussion in a Little Chef where I sat unhappily listening to more of these facts concerning time and motion, all of which were true. I am not fond of true facts about myself when I have a bee in my bonnet and have decided I am going to do something.

On a television screen in the corner, Tim Henman was losing a tennis match. Outside it was beginning to trickle the warm, claustrophobic rain of summer. The covers were dragged over Wimbledon's centre court as Henman made his exit. Sporting events are the easiest way for me to mark time. This is how I can calculate that six months elapsed before I felt it was time for another crack at the subject.

***

Trezza had let the matter rest, it was me who was agitating. I would flick *The Giant Book of the Dog* occasionally in the spirit of provocation, but still nothing was said. And then one day I had the obvious lateral thought: what was needed was not a Vizsla puppy or a puppy of any other sort. Rather, instead, we should seek out a mature animal. I decided that a pensioned-off greyhound would be perfect.

The retired racer, I had learned, from a conversation I'd had with a fellow dog walker while I was out with Mingus, does not require too much in the way of exercise. After the life it has known, it is more than delighted not to have been shot by the barbarian who has previously 'cared' for it, and is content to restrict itself to an easy stroll once or twice a day. For the rest of the time it is happy to mind its own business and lie in the comfort of an old blanket doing absolutely bugger all.

I had come up with a scheme, and I rehearsed my case: a greyhound would allow the new owner an opportunity to take some fresh air once a day while appreciating the changing scenes of nature, a subject about which *she* actually gives a fig. Otherwise she can continue to enjoy a quiet life at home while her partner is who-knows-where doing who-knows-what, but whatever it is, at least he will not be abandoning his puppy-training duties.

From his point of view, a greyhound is something of

a thoroughbred: It is only over recent years that I have come to really love horse racing, and by extension, racehorses. They are a new but consuming passion. I form attachments to them, sometimes I video a race where I haven't even placed a bet just for the pleasure of seeing, say, Azertyuiop and Moscow Flyer – the two fastest chasers around at the time – do battle over two miles and a dozen fences. On those fabulous occasions where I've taken the bookies to the cleaners I rewind the final fences or furlongs and re-watch the finish. But, unless I move into Vizsla breeding, I can't see myself owning a racehorse.

There's no way I'm going to get into greyhound racing either: first, I know next to nothing about it, but, second, I know enough about sport to take an informed guess that the dogs is not something you ought to consider dabbling with in mid-life. The pros will identify you as a clueless amateur in less time than it takes the hare to complete a circuit; it's odds on you'll be bankrupt faster than you can tear up a betting slip.

Additionally, the little I do know about dog racing leads me to the view that it is an activity involving a sizeable number of persons who are not very nice. I have popped into a bookies once in a while to monitor the performance of my considered investment in the 2.35 at Folkestone and found myself in the company of the weekday gamblers, those stalwarts who bet on race after race after race. The dogs go off somewhere around the country every five minutes and, as they do, men gamble and smoke while fixed on television screens.

They seldom celebrate a success (because they are always chasing losses, of course) and with the dogs you will only ever hear the animal referred to by number, never by name, except when it gets called a piece of shit, or worse, simply because it has cost someone another fiver.

It's pretty distasteful. As far as animals go, I'm a sentimentalist and, as far as horse racing goes, there's a lot of that about — it's one of the few sports in which, at the track at least, you can see a loser welcomed back home with as much affection and appreciation as a winner. So here is the ulterior motive in the new scheme: owning a retired greyhound will allow me a stake in a surrogate racehorse whose every run will be virtual, who will always win, who will delight the crowd as he makes all up to the post, adding another victory to his great unbeaten sequence.

This part I don't mention to Trezza. The rest of the 'plan' I sell without too much resistance.

***

There are three greyhounds at the NCDL rescue cen-tre when we visit on the winter's afternoon. They live together in a single pen, but two are spoken for and the third is away being seen by a vet. They live along a bright corridor, together with many other dogs in many other pens. Here I learn something about Trezza: she had a specialised lunatic streak. She wants to take them all home with her.

I was much more circumspect as I regarded the assortment of desperados banged up doing porridge. The scars, half-tails, missing ears and sometimes missing legs, told their own stories. And you could certainly see how some of them had been abandoned, too – you'd put your hand down and they'd have a go at biting it off even through the reinforced glass of the pen. But, alongside the hard cases and the lifers, there were also the pensioners, the wallflowers, the abandoned débutantes; and alongside these were the aristocrats fallen on hard times, the pedigree for which you'd normally expect to hand over the six hundred quid.

It was a pair of Deerhounds to which Trezza gravitated. 'Aren't they beautiful?' she said. I wasn't prepared to go along with this, for while they may or may not have been attractive animals, their pre-eminent characteristic was their height. No doubt *The Giant Book of the Dog* would say they were first-class pets who were superb with children, and no doubt for a certain sort of child they would be worth trying out for a donkey ride. I made no reply concerning the question of beauty, I simply pointed to a little sign which said that, in a perfect world, you would need a paddock or a small field in which to keep them as they had previously belonged to a gamekeeper, and had lived the outdoor life. At home we have a side passage with a bit at the back. The best you could say for this area is that it is a yard.

We were about to leave, having failed to agree on the ideal candidate, when one of the women who worked at the centre approached. She had been observing us and the animals beside which we had lingered longest and she asked if it was a hound we were particularly looking for. We considered this question and said yes, we supposed we probably were.

'I've got a very deserving case in the back,' she said. 'He's four months old. Would you consider a lurcher puppy?'

Notwithstanding the dispute at the Little Chef, it was one of those situations where you cannot say, 'No.' *No, I do not think we would consider a lurcher puppy.* What sort of callous bastards would come out with that? We sat on seats in the foyer waiting for the deserving case to arrive.

His entrance was sudden. He came from a side door pulling the woman along behind him. How he managed this I could only guess. If Giacometti made a sculpture of a new-born deer, this animal could easily have been his model. His coat was predominantly black with off-set fawn highlights down the fronts of his legs and the back of his tail, as well as on either side of his nose, under his chin, and along his chest.

The effect of all this chiaroscuro was to make him look like his own shadow. His face was equine with fawn eyebrows. His tail was ridiculous, longer than his body. He scrambled onto my lap and gave my face a wash before jumping over to provide the same service for Trezza.

'What's his name?' we asked.

'Ernie,' said the woman. 'Cute, isn't he? Would you like to take him for a walk?'

The light dusting of snow was frosting over, so Ernie was issued with an extra-small dog-jacket in order that he could cope with being outside. We were given a plastic bag in case he had any 'little accidents', and together we set off down the lane. Ernie did not seem to be very experienced at going for a walk. He would head in any direction; sideways, backwards, onwards, it was all the same to him. His pronounced legginess made him very gangly; he was something of an expert at getting tangled up in the lead. The NCDL woman had said that the vet had thought he might have rickets when he first arrived, which was a couple of months earlier, but that once he'd been put on a high protein diet he seemed all right in this specific respect. With the way he walked, though – as if he'd never really tried it before – it must have been diffi-cult to tell.

Ernie had been delivered to Snetterton in the dog wardens' van; they had found him in Thetford Forest. He was reckoned to be about eight weeks of age then (not much older than those Vizsla puppies we had visited) and was lucky to have survived at all: it was November when he was picked up – a month when the weather is not ideal for a puppy to be out and about taking care of itself, particularly one built along his supermodel lines.

Not far into our walk Ernie paused and took a dump which could have been nominated for Most Stinking in East Anglia and was not pleasant in appearance either.

'That's a bit much, coming from a boy of his size,' I said. 'Fuck me, what will they be like when he grows up?'

'They'll be fine,' Trezza replied. The way she said this, I could tell that she had unilaterally over-ruled her objections to puppy ownership.

We walked on a little further until Ernie began to look nervously over his shoulder as the smells and sounds of the rescue centre receded. He concentrated more now on pulling backwards than he did sideways or onwards. It was getting colder and dusk was falling so we turned him round, not least to assuage his evident fears. He caught himself up in the lead many more times on the way back, tripping me more than once; at the gates of the centre I picked him up to return him into the care of the woman by hand.

This was in order that I might not look like the sort of rank outsider who was incapable of taking a puppy for a walk without flattening him. As I made to pass him over he squirmed back towards me. I took him and tried tickling his ears but he squirmed towards my face in order to resume the job of giving me a wash.

'Are you interested?' the woman said. We had discussed this matter as we retraced our steps.

'Yes,' Trezza replied, 'We are.'

THE NOBLE LURCHER

After we'd driven back home I fished out *The Giant Book of the Dog* and searched for lurcher in the index. The lurcher was not an animal that had been on my short list before the Vizsla-hunt began, and it had not been on my long list either. In truth, I had no idea what a lurcher was.

I found the details in a classification at the end of the formal breed-by-breed headings; this section was for Rare Breeds. The lurcher was listed in the Rare Breed subsection: Unclassified. A vaguely (but only vaguely) Ernie-like animal was pictured next to the description. The picture was captioned:

The lurcher may have originated in Ireland. It is an excellent poacher's dog, able to run down prey swiftly and silently.

Useful, I thought. Those copses and meadows I had visited with Mingus must be full of rabbits. I imagined us coming home with our quarry tied up in a bag slung over my shoulder, ready to be cooked with wine and onions and garlic.

The lurcher was third-last in the Unclassifieds, ahead of the New Guinea Singing Dog, but behind the Dingo. I felt this was unfair. The general description given was shorter than for the full pedigrees, too, a bit throwaway, further diminishing the standing of this distinguished animal. I shook my head, though I could see there was a certain appropriateness in all of this. From the few words that were written, I discovered that the lurcher was thought to have come into being because at one time in England only those of noble blood were permitted to own a greyhound. To get round this rule a greyhound-cross was developed as *'an efficient poaching dog for a commoner to keep.'*

If we had found the animal for us — and we had — I had certainly found the animal for me. I had already solved the mystery of Ernie's early life by combining the words, 'Thetford Forest,' 'poacher,' and 'rickets,' to come up with the hypothesis that he had been slung out as the runt of a traveller's litter. (Still, at least they didn't park him on the fast lane of the M11.) And now here was *The Giant Book of the Dog* — available for a fiver in the bargain bin at B&Q, and evidently not to be trusted (the lurcher, needless to say, makes a faithful and affectionate family pet) — relegating the status of my Ernie to *commoner*, indeed.

I thrive on having something to resent. The grim circumstances of Ernie's beginnings combined with the marginal status accorded to his kind (and their keepers) provided adequate fuel to keep me nicely chippy. It could only be a matter of time before I was looking at a Vizsla owner through the eyes of the inverted snob.

ANYTHING BUT ERNIE

A number of criteria had to be satisfied before we were allowed to become Ernie's owners. A date was arranged in order that an NCDL staff member could visit us to establish that our garden was secure; they are understandably anxious not to encourage any quick returns among the animals they release. I installed fencing panels at the back of our yard where before there had only been bushes. This dealt with security, but it didn't make the place look any bigger, nor did it make it a garden. We were worried that we might not be allowed to take Ernie at all; we had been deliberately vague when certain questions were put to us at the rescue centre – we had allowed the impression to be formed that our property had some sort of adjoining land.

During the pre-homecoming period we visited Ernie twice more. On each occasion he was delighted to see us, though I don't think he knew who we were, we were just humans. At this time it seemed to me that it seemed to him that humans were a good thing – they allowed him a break in his routine, they fed him treats, not to mention the fact that they gave him the chance to escape from his kennel mate, Martin. Martin was also a lurcher pup, this one a more typical brindle collie-cross, and a born pugilist.

On our second visit we shared some time in the common room with Martin and his new owner-to-be, and for a while Martin treated Ernie to the rough stuff. But, though Ernie was the embodiment of slightness (there seemed to be even less of him now than the first time we saw him), he did not take it lying down. His main technique was to shadow box, but occasionally he'd use his superior agility to go in over the top and sink his teeth into his tormentor's neck. As a tough, he looked about as convincing as a sparrow, but as a dog he seemed more than capable of looking after himself.

Inspection day arrived. By now we were certain that Ernie was our boy (the follow-up visits only served to increase our initial affection for him). We grew anxious that our place would fail the test, that we would not be allowed to bring him home. 'You can have a baby without going through this sort of scrutiny,' we were neurotically saying, to anyone who might be interested.

Our yard has a single French window opening onto it from the dining-room, and folding patio doors which open onto it from a lean to at the rear. We propped all these back, as well as opening all of the rest of the doors in the house as well, to try to create the illusion that what you had here was a huge space for a dog to frolic in. Just before the inspector was due to arrive, we put the coffee on, like estate agents advise. The woman came in, smiled at us, talked about the weather, ticked the box saying the garden was secure, and that was that. The whole thing was a formality (though she did nod in a significant way, saying that not everyone bothers to make the follow-up visits to the rescue centre).

She spent the rest of the time wondering which piece of furniture Ernie would choose to wreck first. She looked sadly at the dining chairs and even more sadly at a leather sofa. Other than that she talked enthusiastically about her own dogs, of which there were five, the most recent of which was a foxhound that had managed to make its way from Liverpool to Kings Lynn (she knew its provenance by the tattoo it had in its ear.)

'I'd have them all if I could,' she said, meaning that she'd take the entire contents of the dogs' home back to her place.

'Yes, me, too, so would I,' Trezza replied, as the coffee was poured. I shut my ears to all this cracked talk.

Jack, my son, who was fourteen, came along to Snetterton to collect the new arrival. Jack had already been out with us on one of the visits. There was a cartoon aspect to Ernie – when he pricked his ears, which he did all the time, his eyebrows shot up. In this way he often looked startled, and bat-like. His Martin-fighting technique, which he interrupted with his wash-your-face routine, and his general

Bambi-ness, together with the bat-like countenance, all led Jack to the view that Ernie was excellent. We paid the compulsory £75 contribution and some extra fees to do with insurance, and Ernie said good-bye to all his friends amongst the staff who seemed genuinely sad to see him go. He'd been neutered during the period we'd been waiting for the all clear (an NCDL stipulation), and one of the young girls who worked there had said that even the vet had been sorry to perform the operation, the implication being that he had good potential as a dad (or at stud, as we dog owners say). We took him across the carpark on his regulation-issue yellow and black NCDL lead and matching collar. (The NCDL has been re-named the Dogs Trust, incidentally – I much prefer the older title with its militant essence and its barmy note of 'Freedom For Tooting'. The leads and collars are still yellow and black, though, and some people keep them for ever, as a code for identifying each other.)

Trezza had filled the back seats of the car with quilts and rugs and blankets for the journey back to Norwich. They'd told us Ernie was a good traveller, in the sense that he wasn't car sick, and they were right, he didn't throw up; neither did he use any of the quilts, rugs or blankets, choosing instead to remain safe on Jack's lap where he sat looking very, very worried, as if he was too nervous to puke.

***

When I was a young boy in the early Seventies the comedian Benny Hill released a novelty song (the musical equivalent of a shih tzu with ribbons in its hair poking out of a bimbo's handbag). Hill's novelty song achieved the distinction of becoming a chart-topping number one hit single. As someone once said, 'Nobody ever lost money by underestimating the taste of the British Public.'

Hill's record was a tale about a milkman who is thwarted in love by a bread roundsman. The milk-man's name, and the title of the song, was *Ernie*. The chorus went: '*Ernie* [backing singer echo, Ernie], *And he drove the fastest milkcart in the west.*'

I had been singing and whistling this tune, complete with the backing singer echo, at regular intervals ever since we had been introduced to our new pet. The circumstances of his arrival at the Snetterton dogs' home, one of the unnumbered, meant that his name had been given to him by the staff from their stock of off-the-shelf dog names. We were not satisfied with it. For one it didn't suit his personality, and for two my singing of the execrable song was driving the missus round the bend and was not good for my own mental health either. To avoid any extra confusion for the poor animal in his already confused young life, we searched for a substitute name that sounded similar. I was all for Bjarni, after one of my favourite football players. Trezza said I would feel differently once Bjarni had transferred from Stoke City to Sampdoria, and that additionally there was no way she was shouting *that* in the park.

And so, after various other unsuitable footballer's names had been eliminated, along with other unsuitable sporting names (Me: 'Desert Orchid'? Trezza: 'NO'), or even the names that were unconnected with any significant sport, names that were good names, but not appropriate for him – Monty, for example – Trezza came up with the idea of calling him after a famous orphan, what with him being an orphan himself and all.

I've heard that there's a musical called *Oliver!* If by

any chance the production features a 'number' that goes: *'Ollie* [backing singer echo, *Ollie*], *And he asked for more gruel, the little pest,'* I remain unaware of it because I loathe musicals (compilations of novelty songs) more than almost anything in the world. Therefore I won't be seen singing and whistling an off-key version of any such unspeakable ditty.

The re-christened pup

WALKING OLLIE

On arriving at his new home, the re-christened pup ran about the place looking worried (he could run and look worried at the same time). After a good bit of this running and worrying, he took a flying leap into a bed in the corner of the lounge that had been prepared for his arrival.

The bed was a nest of rugs finished with a sheepskin throw. He sat on the throw, and the worried look remained, but he settled a little as we hand-fed him slices of sausage, warm chicken breast, and cubes of thick bacon, tempted him to play with cuddly toys with squeakers, and generally made a fuss of him.

The story should end here, really, and end happily ever after, too, with Ollie breaking his teeth in on the furniture while becoming ever more relaxed and content and less worried-looking. That's how I thought it would be. Though I knew, in the abstract way, that there was work to be done, I thought that living with Ollie would be the same as bringing up a child, only a lot easier. I imagined that he would turn out like Mingus, that after our walks together he would sit in the kitchen observing and sniffing, and that soon enough he would love and respect me even without the price of half a pork pie, because I would be his Master and he would be my Faithful Companion.

But Ollie is a rescue dog. As you talk to more and more dog owners, certain truths dawn on you and they dawn on you fast. The main truth, of which there are many sub-truths, is that rescue dogs are always problematical and deranged in the head. You get to hear plenty about the multiple manifestations of the derangements that exist because rescuers are amongst the most verbose of owners. Rescuers will purge at the drop of a hat; it's a form of therapy. Their accounts are by no means easy to follow either, because rescue dogs often have stories to tell that are even more complicated and convoluted than those you hear on Jerry Springer.

And, of course, the animal itself cannot talk, so something is always lost in translation. Dogs have to be spoken for, that is their chief lack, and I think they know it. Some of them may want to be human, some of them certainly don't, but given the chance I think they'd all speak up from time to time. They supply a certain, and sometimes urgent, amount of information through body language and eye contact of course, but the rest we are obliged to make up, flesh out and elaborate into a Hollywood-style production. The outcome of all this is that many dogs are anthropomorphised: 'She's a bit down today, I can tell by her *aura*.'

Sometimes I get caught up in such an involved narrative at the beginning of our walk, that it's half an hour before we even get started. In the first few months of Ollie, my irritation at the waste of jogging opportunities that these conversations represented went out of the window, as I was forced to evolve a new concept of myself in relation to time. Even at the beginning, when things were relatively normal, I could find that I had been out in nature for ten hours in a single week – an incursion greater than a day's work.

My first thoughts were along the lines of compensatory shifts in the evenings, in order to preserve the concept of the payroll, the working week/weekend divide which is in any event difficult to maintain when you are a writer because there is so much on offer in the way of distraction, displacement, and messing about. But evening shifts could not be made to fit as there is sport to be played and watched, there are soaps, there may be socialising, drinking, and there is always idling to be taken into account once six o'clock has arrived. As time went on, and dog-creep started to erode time that should have been designated for these other activities, I made the adjustment that was easiest to make. I cut down on soaps.

Sometimes I went to bed early in order to be up earlier to get the walk out of the way, but our best walking areas are far enough from home to necessitate a drive – early morning traffic doesn't help, coffee bars beckon – there seemed to be no real gain there. So, in short, I assimilated this new time spent dog-walking as best I could: I simply wrote it off.

On top of the specific erosion of time, there were

dog-creep adjustments that affected our life together: we took fewer weekend breaks (because kennelling seems cruel), did less in the way of going to the pub for the early drink, because we're busy (walking the dog), and experienced a drastic cut-back in eating out. But then, what sort of restaurant would want us? Post-Ollie, unless it's a really special occasion, I seldom bother with clean clothes. They only get immediately re-coated in dog hair and stuff, there's no point. Much less is there anything to be said for ironing them. Instead I keep my 'wardrobe' in a heap on a chest under the bedroom window, and wear it over and over again as each item comes back to the top of the pile on a rotation system which means I only need to use the washing machine about once a quarter.

As the first flush of Ollie-owning began to go awry and I took my own therapy from other dog walkers, I got to hear many tales of failed cases. It was helpful; seeing and hearing about animals who had behaviour syndromes to rival those that were developing in my own case gave me some perspective. Often I never even saw the dog in question because it had been returned to a rescue centre — a consequence of its unmanageability, cracked habits, insanities and neuroses. In many instances the person telling the story would be walking a different, replacement animal, with different difficulties.

The biggest single problem is destruction – there are many dogs out there who are into it in a big way, who will be guaranteed to smash the place up as soon as a back is turned. I heard of dogs who simply would not never stop barking (that would drive me insane). I heard of dogs who shook their heads violently so that drool was constantly flying about and sticking to the ceiling. Repulsive. I heard of dogs who had been perfectly peaceable until one day they caught sight of an animal which, on the face of things, was just like any other dog they'd encountered before, but to which they had taken a sudden dislike, and of how they had attacked, and drawn blood and caused damage. And then how they had done it again. And being muzzled sent them into a frenzy. So they had to be put down.

Once or twice I heard the same story related to attacks on people, and on one occasion I heard about a dog that had turned on its owners and really terrified them (this one wasn't even a rescue). I heard of dogs who, if they were left alone for five minutes, would develop a routine that began with simple crying and howling, then before anyone knew it they'd be digging up the floorboards while spraying pee and poo about the place in a full-scale dirty protest.

Why do people put up with this? They are not all rescue owners, so sometimes the answer is because six hundred quid (or more) has been shelled out, and the purchaser is trying to make some sort of sense out of that investment; sometimes it is because the owner is a saint, and sometimes they don't put up with it: this is the way in which certain animals are recycled through the rescue centres, those lifers and hard cases I had already seen.

Then there were the dogs who went missing, for days on end, who could never ever be allowed off the lead with any confidence. I met a man in a deserted pine forest one Thursday afternoon who had such an animal reined in close. He told me he'd let it off once this one time years back, and that it had disappeared; two weeks later someone had found it in their back garden, fifteen miles away. His wife had been frantic. So now he didn't let the animal loose at all, ever, it was too risky, see. The dog didn't like him really, he said. It only responded to his wife (it was a low, unprepossessing mutt too, not that this counts a jot once a bond has been made). His wife had to cajole the dog to go out with him at all, it wouldn't follow him to the front door or anything, whereas it perked up no end if it saw her gathering together her outdoor clothes. He shook his head at this, though he appeared to harbour the animal no resentment; he just seemed sad.

You expect dogs to be frightened on Bonfire Night, but then I heard of dogs who were frightened of rain, of umbrellas, of wheelbarrows, and of shopping bags. Ollie has Shopping Bag Syndrome. Wind is a constant worry, it may come from anywhere, unannounced – a flapping shopping bag is the wind made solid. Flies upset him, especially if they circle a lightshade. Emergency vehicles sounding sirens freak him out – though fireworks, in fact, make no impact. Coats hanging on the backs of doors spook him most of all. I think they must remind him of a nasty man, as, in time, I came to do.

Complete novice and incompetent dog-handler that I was, like a new parent I was determined to do it all without any outside assistance, safe in the knowledge that everything I was doing was right, and for the best.

There was still snow – it was still winter, late

January – when Ollie arrived, so we bought him the smallest waxed, sheepskin-lined dog jacket we could find. Even this was a bit too big, and when we fastened it on he was quick to attack it because of the limitations it imposed on his walking technique. It was me who wanted to get him house-trained as soon as possible (my tolerance for coming downstairs in the morning to a pissy, shitty stench is low) so it was me who took him for a tour round the block last thing at night in the hope that he would do his business, and that this would see him through until morning. He didn't much care for these excursions, and here, I think, was the seed of where we started to go wrong.

During our very first walk together, back at Snetterton, I suppose he had thought (does a dog think? I don't know; they are certainly capable of *looking* thoughtful) that he was having to do this stupid thing just this once, that the humans would see how hopeless he was at it, and that it wouldn't happen again. As it became a regular activity, he began to dread it. He pulled, he tried to run, he flinched, he backed up, he practically reared. He cowered against the front walls of houses, his tail so far in between his legs that it touched his chest. We got into such tangles that he would end up half-throttling himself with the lead. None of this was good; I may have known nothing, but I knew that. I had heard of puppy training classes and socialisation groups and soon I would be taking him along to these, or so I planned. I attempted to prepare him for the idea by tugging the lead back a little when he was pulling the most and saying, 'Heel,' frequently and repeatedly.

Our house is situated amongst main roads and not far from the train station. Ollie went into this night-time world coatless (it was worn twice; aside from cramping his style, the sight of it became a signal to him that bad things were about to happen) – ergo he was not warm; in addition there was frightening traffic, the sound of moving trains, hoots from the trains that came from nowhere like wind does; and to top it all there was the idiot man repeatedly making a sound that meant nothing to him whatsoever (even now I think Ollie understands very few words, and that if he could speak it would be in some arcane Egyptian-Romany dialect). And, just to put the tin lid on all the bad karma, he was repeatedly having his throat hoiked at.

So far as Ollie was concerned, the whole night-time-walk concept was a disaster. It took him out of the comfort of a bed in the warm and dry, where he could snuggle into his sheepskin throw with his head down and his paws wrapped over the front of his nose, raising one or the other of his eyebrows and looking worried. I can see this now.

Back then I simply thought that he'd soon get used to it, that a dog – any dog – would naturally opt for a walk at any time of the day or night, because for a dog getting out of the house and into the activity of sniffing around street lamps and gate posts is the absolute business. Any dog. This was my prime miscalculation. Like saying, 'Any human', it's a generalisation that doesn't work. Some humans like going for a walk and some don't, and some like going for a walk sometimes, but not at other times. They are not all the same, this is the point.

Additionally I was operating in a world of assumption that was based on the premise that Ollie must be counting himself lucky, that he had done well to be sprung from the NCDL centre, out of the way of that irritating little prick Martin, and into an environment where he was kept snug and cared for, fed, given toys, and played with and loved. It never crossed my mind to think that perhaps he hadn't much wanted to leave Snetterton because he liked it there, that Martin was actually a close personal friend, that their love-hate relationship was the way it suited them, or that our house could represent some sort of confinement since it was not a forest or a dog-pen where he was free to do as he wanted, how and when he saw fit, and to express himself in his own way. No, none of this ever occurred to me back then, but it has occurred to me since.

So, from the outset, albeit that it might have been born of good intentions, I was responsible, with that night-time walking stuff, for creating a bit of an atmosphere between us.

***

If you acquire a pup in the more usual manner, weaned at eight weeks from the breeder, common advice you'll be given is not to let it off the lead until it's about four months old (or more, depending on breed) as its legs won't be strong enough for the running about in which it will inevitably indulge. In Ollie's case, because he'd been free to roam since before he was two months old, here was a protocol he'd never observed.

I thought about this. His limbs had come through it fine. He could shift about the house in style if the mood took him, he would race up the stairs to see what was what and be back down in a flash — on the run from a flapping curtain or a terrifying mystery object like a sudden ironing board. He'd perform a triple lutz of some originality to land himself back onto the safety of his bed. So his body was fit, but what about his mind? He did not like restriction. The coat, the lead: for him they were both equally wrong. If the night-time walks weren't going too well, surely the daytime experience could be made better?

We began to explore the open spaces around us where he could be allowed some limited freedom. I discovered a variation on a meadow — a paddock — a meadow with a fence around it. We carried out basic 'training' in the paddock using one of those retractable leads: we established that he would come to our call/hand for certain treats above and beyond sausages, for example lambs' liver or cheddar cheese. This treat diet precipitated the sort of farts you could slice and dice, it was beyond me that a stomach and bowel contained within the slenderness of his waist could produce nerve gas like that. Still, outdoors at least you could move away from the pong, after a fashion: having him at the end of the extension lead was like trying to take a ferret for a walk — disentangling him from the infinite number of variants he could find for getting himself into knots was a full time job in itself.

'For fuck's sake, let's just let him off shall we?'

This is me suggesting the way forward. Fannying about in a meadow like this was exposing my patience threshold in all its dismal short-temperedness. So we did let him off. And, though he wasn't at all brilliant at coming back or responding to any sort of instruction signalled by our whistling, calling, or changing the pitch of our voices, the freedom clearly delighted him.

Liberated from the lead, he relaxed; you could see his worries disappear. I watched him as he shot past us. Where indoors he would run and look worried at the same time, out here he could run and smile. He did a figure of eight, a loop the loop, the hop, skip and jump, any number of fifty-metre sprints, and several circuits. It was the first time I'd seen him happy since his arrival; it was clear in an instant that running was his vocation in life. So, to try and help build our bond, which had seemed fragile from the moment we left Snetterton (I noticed from the very beginning that he shied slightly from me, looking to Trezza for reassurance), I started to allow him off the lead at night too, in the carpark at the back of Carrow Road, Norwich City's football ground.

This is also near to where we live, and was an area

Worries disappear, for one of us at least

that I was incorporating into our evening outings. Trezza would have been horrified if she had known, because of the roads nearby. But I was concerned to improve the quality of life on the emptying tour (just because *he* wasn't keen, it didn't stop *me* from carrying on).

First, I conducted experiments with the extension lead, which taught me that his behaviour on a span of tarmac was quite different to that in a paddock. Where the grass seemed to tickle his feet and have him drop the turbo, here his tendency was to the dainty: he trotted, like a ballerina. Slower, see. And more considered. I kept close by him once I'd set him free, though sometimes he would stray out of reach, and once out of reach he might keep himself at that distance, then stop, and look at me quizzically as I offered him the chicken which I'd picked off the bone on the way out.

He would sit considering the matter; was the food/possible-return-to-lead trade-off worth it? His appetite always won, and while he was eating out of one hand I would take hold of his collar with the other.

Having done what we came to do, we would walk

back through the scary streets with the scary noises, back over the scary railway bridge, Ollie pulling furiously and me tugging him back and saying 'Heel' to no effect at all. Even having completed his night-time businesses I would invariably wake in the morning to find more. Where did it all come from?

***

As I'd mentioned to the Vizsla lady, Trezza and I both work from home. In the daytime I took to wandering downstairs from my office more often than was necessary to look in on Ollie, to see if he was all right. I'd find him sitting nervously on, or under, his throw, or in his other basket in the dining-room (it had been decided that he needed a selection of beds). Never particularly keen, as time went on he welcomed me less. He didn't seem to like me coming into his space. And he didn't seem to like being looked at, either. He would turn his face towards the wall and cast occasional neurotic glances backwards to see if I was still there, as though he hoped I'd be gone. If I approached him to tickle him under his chin, he edged away. I'd try stroking his back, which went down no better. I couldn't work him out. Shouldn't he be delighted every time I showed up? After all, it could mean food or an excursion.

Ollie didn't seem normal. That said, in the first few days and weeks, I felt the whole idea was abnormal anyway – having this weird creature in our house, our living space. Beyond the unfamiliarity, it seemed wrong. His claws tip-tapping over the floorboards made an odd percussion that disturbed me. His permanent nervous presence created a bad vibe. We'd get our paths crossed and I'd trip over him, or vice-versa. Worse, I'd tread on his tail and make him yelp; he'd back off looking more than his usual worried self, looking genuinely fearful, and when I'd try to stroke him to say sorry, he'd back further off.

We didn't seem to know how to deal with each other at all. I wondered what on earth I'd been thinking about, bringing a wild animal into the house. I'd lived with cats before but cats really do mind their own business: you simply install the cat flap, the rest is down to them. With Ollie, I felt responsible. I should have seen that he was in some kind of distress, maybe, but I didn't interpret him that way. In my impatient inexperience I thought that he was being a bit dense, that what he needed to do was to sort himself out. I was surprised that in trying the obvious, the reassurance of gentle touching, I was not getting through. Rather the opposite. He remained significantly more relaxed with Trezza, and when Jack turned up he actually wagged, a signal of happiness that we never saw.

All the same, I imagined he'd come round, in the end. I would remove myself from his sightline – so as not to upset him by looking at him – and observe him through the crack between door and frame, a surveillance that allowed me to note that he wasn't much better in my absence: occasionally, he'd put his head down and sigh; otherwise he spent his whole time looking around nervously at all the things that alarmed him – the curtain, the windowpane that might rattle if any wind came, the lampshade – no doubt all the while dreading the reappearance of the scary fly.

**

After a couple of weeks of the outdoor training with short runs in the paddock, we set out on our first big off-lead session in the parkland to the south side of the

University of East Anglia. I don't recall much about it, which must mean it was a more or less incident-free day, which would have made it a very untypical outing. Sometimes we walked him together, but soon fell into a routine where I did the morning and Trezza the later one; in the first weeks we compared notes on Ollie's ways.

There are other parks in Norwich, but the land to the south side of the campus is by far the biggest open space, a few hundred acres consisting of copse, rough fields, sports pitches, a river, and a lake. The river is separated from the sports pitches by a long hedge with stiles, the copses are scattered throughout, and footpaths run at angles. A couple of bridges cross the river, one a footbridge, the other a single lane university road (the road where we met the whippet in the preface). This road is mainly used by cycling fascists who yield to no one (I have grown to loathe this sector of society even more than I do musicals: no other group contains quite such an over-representative sample of sanctimonious, sixth-form, wholegrain prats). As well as the two-wheeled fascists, the road is trafficked by speeding tractors pulling grass-cutters, and an excess of foreign students on foot passing between their lessons and residences. The foreign students tend to be wary of dogs, the vehicles and the two-wheeled fascists less so. There may be matches taking place on the pitches, and there are many joggers. Occasionally you come across lovers who are up to something, and, in good weather, groups of partying teenagers. The University Goths' Sword Fencing & Dressing-up Society is often to be seen re-enacting a moment from myth.

These are the principal hazards that may impede Ollie while he is pursuing his lifetime's ambition: to personally greet every other dog in the world. Once he's off the lead he's away to his nearest brother as quickly as possible, which is quick. Many people take him for a greyhound and ask if we race him, which is a fair mistake to make.

Even in his early stages when he was still slight and immature he was no slouch; as he grew he became a rocket. And as he did not seem to be a normal dog in the head, neither was his running style conventional. Before he put his ears back and really gathered some steam, his warm-up consisted of bouncing. Boing, boing, boing. Then he'd stop and hang in mid-air – like the fight sequences in *The Matrix* – while he assessed the lie of the land. On touchdown he ran beautifully, his body elastic, his technique effortless. To say he flew over the ground would be accurate. I noticed people stop and turn to watch, even people without a dog, even nervy foreign students.

As he neared his object-dog, his normal method was to scorch the grass in an emergency stop, pulling up short, and hunching down with his stomach flat to the ground, hind legs tucked in, front legs splayed in front. If you wanted a study of an Anubis, this was the moment. Head half-up, half-down, ears pricked, body trembling with excitement, he waited to see what on earth would happen next. Or sometimes not. Sometimes he didn't pull up short, sometimes he just sledged straight in around the back of the object-dog, opened his jaws and put them round the object-dog's neck.

This, I came to understand, is his way of saying, 'C'mon baby! Chase me.' But there are owners who tend to misinterpret it as an attack. If I can see their point of view these days, I was less happy with their general attitude back when Ollie was clearly a super-lightweight pup who *only wants to play*.

There are some senses in which you feel you never

learn a thing. In so much as I'd given the matter any thought at all, I'd assumed that dog-loving animal lovers would be nice people, loving animals as they do. I had not considered the possible corollary – they keep a dog because they are misanthropic twerps and a dog does not answer back. In the beginning I was a cheerful person, in the way people on holiday are cheerful – I was in a new place doing a new activity, I was out in nature and I was feeling good.

Ollie only wanting to play

However, I found many of my friendly 'Good Mornings' blanked, much more often than you would believe. I was taken aback by how rude country dog-walking folk could be. But never mind me, what about Ollie? If they noticed him at all, it was to shoo him away or to curse him.

Some of these other owners don't love animals either, with the sole exception of their own ball-fixated Border collie-cross. (Border collie-cross owners tend to confuse their animals' obsessive natures with Good Behaviour. And any dog that is not like theirs falls a long way short of the standard; they will glower at you down the barrel of their nose to leave you in no doubt about this.)

While border collie-cross owners may be the pre-eminent School Ma'ms in the world of dog control, decorum, and manners, there are many other examples to be taken into account. There were three old boys who patrolled together, one in camouflage gear, another with a Union Jack t-shirt, the third their Sherpa. This self-proclaimed 'People's Army' had three trusty old hounds to go with them. Though I was on the same shift, and saw them every day, they never once acknowledged Ollie's efforts to play with these dogs, who were every bit as standoffish as their owners. The interpretation was simple. Worse than new kids in the playground, we were invading their land. Moreover, we lacked discipline. I continued to put in my unacknowledged 'Good Mornings', to agitate them, to set their nostrils twitching above their Kitchener moustaches. Still, at least they didn't pick their dogs up, like some, or put them back on the lead, like others, as soon as they caught sight of Ollie.

Owners became the bane of my life. Not dogs, who, in the main, were superb. Left to its own devices even the most pumped-up, steroid-abusing Staffordshire Bull Terrier sporting the studded collar and nose ring would offer Ollie a playful snarl, a Colgate smile, and twenty terrifying laps snapping at his hindquarters just for a laugh. Breeds with reputations to live up to – Dobermanns, Rottweilers, Ridgebacks – all turned out to be pussycats once you got to know them: chasing the new boy, tipping him upside down and giving him a bit of a kicking was right up their street, especially as the fool kept coming back for more. *I* was more scared of these animals than Ollie was.

To be fair and accurate, a good number of owners were more than fine, too. But it wasn't long before I was giving a wide berth both to specific miserablists as well as whole categories of irritant: besides the pickers-up and the putters-on-the-lead, there were the

Thatcherite disciplinarians ('No, no, no, no no no no – Niet!'), the aloof, and the snooty ('I didn't pay a fortune for this pedigree to have it associate with the likes of *you*'). Principal amongst these stiffs were the pairs you only ever see on Saturday and Sunday (like traffic jams at retail parks, dog-walking peaks at the weekend).

The pairs of stiffs come in all ages, but they are easy to identify as they arrive in uniform: His 'n Hers Observer-Special-Offer Wellington boots, beige chinos for him, beige jodhpurs for her, a Barbour jacket apiece with the little rectangular Barbour Prefect badges pinned on the breasts, and Lady Di scarves for both, all brand new and starched. They walk a shampooed Labrador or golden retriever and they walk it in a curious, dainty manner, because in their private universe they are in the Main Ring at Crufts having just retained the Supreme Champion of Champions Rosette for the third successive year. Their dog is never allowed off the lead. Sometimes it's not a retriever; instead it's a Wiemaraner.

I don't know why they bother, why they don't just settle for a couple of mountain bikes instead. One thing is for certain: they do not want some reprobate like Ollie ruining their day by trying to be friendly. He was – he is – very persistent. And equally disobedient. So far as he is concerned, the words, 'Ollie: Stop' and 'Ollie:No!' are amongst the most meaningless in the language. Attempting to catch hold of his collar while he sledges little Freddy, apparently taking chunks of fur out of his neck, is a nightmare – like trying to tickle trout and catch soap in the bath all at the same time with one arm tied behind your back. To give little Freddy credit, in most instances *he* at least tends to give the impression that he'd be happy to play the game, if only he knew how, and was a bit fitter – difficult, as this excursion represents his entire week-ly exercise.

As I dive about trying to field Ollie, the stiffs stand, suppressing emotion, while the disgraceful behaviour goes on, and on. And on.

And on.

It could be several long minutes before I actually got hold of the pest, or, much more likely, he would go off in a different direction of his own accord, having been distracted by the sight of his next victim.

At first I'd apologise, but I soon stopped bothering,

because I didn't feel sorry. Here is a public message to all Labrador-Retriever-Observer-Special-Offer Wiemaraner-Wellington-Boot-Couples everywhere: If you're going to have a dog, LET IT PLAY, you odious farts.

But, as the weeks added up to a month, then two months, and the season began to turn, and Ollie still refused to listen to a single word I said, his antics began to wear on me. While he got up to his stuff, I took to pretending I wasn't with him – there are plenty of trees to hide behind in a copse. We thought of obedience classes, obviously, but he was so far short of any sort of standard of behaviour, unresponsive to any command at all, with the possible exception of 'Sit' (providing he was in the mood), that we just didn't think he was ready. In addition, he was an entirely different animal indoors, where I imagined these classes took place. So instead of trying to train him, I grew stubble, wore shades, and dressed to give the impression of being the kind of person you wouldn't want to pick an argument with, or even talk to at all. If I encountered someone new, who wouldn't know it was a lie, I might use the line, 'That's the last time I look after *this* dog,' as though he belonged to a friend. I stopped saying, 'Good Morning', for what it was worth. All the same, I acknowledged to myself that the dog was out of hand, and that realistically something had to be done.

In spite of my appearance, some super-tense owners still mentioned this to me. 'That animal is out of control,' they'd say, in the strangulated whine of the suburban reprimand (the south side of the university is set in a middle-class residential area). I developed my stock answer to this observation.

'He's a rescue, just picked him up, he's only a pup.'

I'd say it as though I were a canine-guru who was putting Ollie through an assessment programme before implementing the appropriate course of home-opathic reprogramming. It would have been nice if this were true, because his non-normality was beginning to exhibit itself in an ever more exaggerated Jekyll and Hyde syndrome: while he was the worst-behaved child in the playground, back home he grew more timid and introverted by the day, especially with me.

Within the walls of our house his plain desire was to become invisible. His body language was getting increasingly poor at any approach I made. Trezza was finding him a strange animal, too, but with her, at least, he was better behaved in public (the notes we compared had me grinding my teeth) and remained marginally more outgoing at home, though context is worth mentioning: as it turned out, he never did wreck any of the furniture – once he'd cased out the scary upstairs, and decided it was out of bounds, he stayed downstairs all day long doing absolutely nothing. He licked the wallpaper off the wall adjacent to his bed, and gnawed at the floorboards around his basket, once in a while he would find a felt pen and make a mess, which could be particularly alarming if it was a red felt pen, giving rise to the momentary thought that he'd done himself in, but that was the worst of it. His indoor routine dictated that he seldom ever actually *moved*. Movement, in its many guises, was a matter strictly reserved for the outdoors.

***

I started to have difficulty getting Ollie to return to me at the end of walks. As he became familiar with the geography of the university grounds, and as we made our way back towards where the car was parked, he began to recognise this as the signal that the best part of his day was about to end. He would drag behind, shoot off at tangents, reappear at a distance and then stop some way short. I would crouch and make cooing noises while offering a hand containing his favourite treat – cubes of Glastonbury Cheddar. He'd stay put. I'd shuffle forward slightly. He'd stay put. I'd draw closer, so he could smell the food. He'd stay put. 'Cheese, Ollie, *cheese*,' I'd say. He'd dive in while executing advanced Matrix manoeuvres involving diving out at the same time.

I began to prepare for these moments and sometimes I'd be sharp enough to catch him with a snatch at his collar, but more often not. When a first attempt failed it became a hugely unfair one-sided game as Ollie stood off and danced back at any advance I made. It was infuriating. Even given my new mindset in relation to time, I still had many better things to do with it.

Sometimes I'd refuse to play, choosing instead to lean against the turnstile at the top of the walk, feeling aggrieved as the other dog-walkers came and went with their obedient animals while Ollie flitted in and out of the trees taunting me. I'd try a few breathing exercises that I'd heard of before my next attempt. The breathing exercises failed: Ollie could sense my tension and would stand even further off.

Fifteen minutes might elapse. I'd feel the beginnings of rage, which I'd repress. I believe dogs can smell repressed rage: his every movement took him away from me. The only method I had left now was to lay a trail of Cheddar and fool him by stretching out an arm, my hand containing a final wedge of cheese, to one side, while coming in from behind for his collar with the other arm, though this wasn't foolproof – he could still sense the incoming movement and escape. Then the whole routine began again, only now Ollie would be on emergency red alert, having nearly allowed himself to be captured twice, and I would be out of cheese.

I could be looking at a half-hour episode before some kind-hearted owner whose dog's behind he had gone to sniff caught hold of him. It was easier for them; they held the element of surprise which I had so completely lost.

I began to dread these moments. I took to dragging Trezza or Jack along with me so that they could retrieve him at the end of the walk, which, just to rub it in, either of them could manage with ease. Trezza could even shout at him to make him compliant. I knew from the one single experiment I'd conducted that to raise my voice was to freak him out and spook him even more. I had not anticipated losing five or six hours a week on top of the actual walking itself to be farted about by an animal who was becoming increasingly wary of me all the time, any time, any place, anywhere, in a manner that was inexplicable. And, additionally, it seemed I had no tools to deal with him. The whole scene was depressing.

***

A friend of Trezza's came to stay. We went to eat in town. On our return, at about ten thirty, I volunteered myself for the night-time empty out.

By now this activity was no longer a daily ritual; as the nights began to draw out we'd started experimenting with taking him for a late evening second walk and skipping last-thing since it didn't seem to be doing any of us any good. I might wake to find a present in the morning, but so what? – picking-up was beginning to slip down my list of Ollie-related problems. Still, on this occasion, I used him as an excuse to be on my own, to clear off out of the way and let the girls' talk begin.

For once I was relaxed, not least on account of the bottle of wine I'd consumed. I walked Ollie down to Carrow Road and let him off in the carpark to attend to his toilet. The one extra reason I could claim for these unauthorised freedoms I was allowing him was that I'd learnt he didn't like relieving himself if you were nearby, and he didn't like being watched while he was at it either, not for poos, that is – he'd piss anywhere, like all dogs. He'd piss when he didn't even need a piss. He didn't cock his leg, he crouched like a girl. Trezza said this was because he'd had his equipment decommissioned too young. Sometimes I had a piss myself, and I'd cock my own leg to try to give him a clue, but he didn't seem to see any connection between human piss and dog piss, much less did he consider my technique.

So I pretended to look away and smoked a cigarette while he did his main business. I bagged and binned the turd. He wandered into the darkness at the far end of the carpark. I called him. He backed off. I threw him a bit of chicken. He ate it and backed off again. We continued this game until we were very close to the front of the stadium. I reversed, to lure him back into the safety of the carpark. But he stayed put. I called him. Nothing.

I whistled him.

Nothing.

'Chicken, Ollie,' I said, '*Chicken!*' I took a step forward and he cantered away round the corner, in the opposite direction, down the service road in front of the main stand, towards the main road proper. This could not be happening because this was the behaviour he reserved for the fields at the university, it was not for here where it had never happened before. I trotted after him, softly calling his name and saying, 'Chicken.' He went faster. I came to a halt, hoping he'd follow suit. He carried on. He'd put an unrecoverable distance between us now and was nearing the three-lane highway that runs parallel to the service road. The highway has phosphorescent orange overhead lighting and is edged by industrial units, a petrol station, and supermarkets. It's not that busy at that time of night, but it's not that quiet either and is the absolute wrong place for a dog with no road sense to be.

In a flash, Ollie was making his way along the middle of this tarmac. I gave full chase now, it was my only option, not that there was a rat's chance of catching him, he could outpace me many times over. He went through a red light, round a bend and towards the railway bridge.

I began to sprint, but even sprinting couldn't take me into his slipstream. We made it over the blind summit of the bridge unscathed. On the other side another road merges as it becomes a one-way system. Cars were coming in from both sides and, as they swerved and slowed, some even pulled up, drivers and passengers trying to coochy-coo him out of danger. They must have wondered what sort of creature had escaped, and from where. He was six months now, three times the size he had been when we picked him up. In the dark he could pass for an antelope. He kept going: no scary person in a scary car was going to fool him with some scary coochy-coo routine. I followed, uphill, round the top of the one-way system. Here it turns into another main road. A few hundred yards on the right is our house. First there's one side road, then a second. Our house is on the corner of the second side road and has an entrance round the back with a hard standing, a space Ollie is familiar with because that's where he jumps in and out of the car four times a day at either end of his walks.

Given that the chase we were having was happening on the opposite side of the one-way system to the route we take on the walk down to Carrow Road — and was therefore new to him — I felt certain he had no idea where he was and that he would miss the turn. This would put us on the road to Great Yarmouth. The fiasco would become a marathon which would end with one, or both, of us spread across the road under the wheels of a truck. Instead, Ollie cornered on the second right, and cornered again, to enter the back of our house through the open door of the conservatory lean-to. I caught up with him as he stood cowering against the French door in the side passage yard where he'd met his dead-end.

To this day I'm convinced the manoeuvre that took him home was accidental. No doubt I should have gone up to him and patted him and told him what a clever boy he was for finding his way back.

However, I did not feel too good after being forced to run a mile, in a panic, through traffic, in the middle of main roads, in the dark, on the back of a warm-up that had consisted of a few fags and a bottle of wine. I smacked Ollie on his nose and I shouted at him. It wasn't that hard a smack, but it wasn't that gentle a smack either. The shouting spoke volumes for all the unshouted words I'd bottled up on the fields of the university.

Trezza appeared, alerted by the commotion. I explained what had happened. This precipitated a stand-up row because, notwithstanding the smack, which was unforgivable, what on earth was I doing letting him off his lead down there in the first place?

'I've been doing it for ages,' I said.

'Then you're an idiot,' she replied.

***

The following morning when I came downstairs Ollie went into a corner with his back up, his coat Mohawked along his spine, and his tail so far between his back legs it was out through his front legs. He looked prehistoric, and he put me in a filthy mood. Suit yourself, I thought. It was you that started it by running away in the first place. I'd had enough. He was only a dog, and he was not going to ruin my life.

Trezza noted my reaction and asked if that was how I was going to deal with the situation, then – by sulking. Did I think a dog would understand sulking?

'What can I do?' I said.

I wished I hadn't hit him but, for crying out loud, was it such an abnormal response? It's only what any person would be driven to. Trezza advised me that he was a poor, sensitive, defenceless creature and asked how I'd feel if I were whacked on the nose by a vicious giant.

'I did it for his own sake,' I said.

'Well he wouldn't really be able to work that out, would he? she replied.

This was exactly what I needed, to be made to feel like a criminal. When a jockey whips a horse towards the finishing post, the commentator calls it a 'reminder'. Does the horse bear the jockey a grudge for this? Not as far as I can tell. I'd seen other owners give their dog a reminder too, on a few occasions. I'd had an old lady clear her cantankerous Jack Russell out of Ollic's way with the toe of her boot. And I'd seen more than a few owners flip out and attempt to control their animal by swinging one at its backside. While it may be unedifying, like seeing a child smacked in a supermarket, I'd noted that, without exception, the dogs had carried on just as before, if not the more so.

But now Ollie remained where he was, trembling

in the corner. I could have kicked him for it. After all, what had I done to deserve his general attitude, his taunting, his running away, his suspicion? Hand-fed him chicken, steak, liver, Glastonbury Cheddar and biscuits, and in between times taken him out to play, that's what.

'Do you ever hit Jack?' Trezza asked, knowing the answer to this was a negative.

'I slapped his hand when he kept trying to put it into the fire when he was two years old,' I said: *for his own protection*. 'For fuck's sake, dogs *do* have to be disciplined, you know.'

'Not like that,' she said.

I went to offer Ollie a conciliatory stroke. He pissed himself on the spot.

***

Though he didn't make a habit of the on-the-spot pissing, and though I simmered down and acted nice in the days that followed, his response to me just got worse and worse. I could sense him flinching before I even entered the house. Once I was in his space he'd slink along the wall, creep into the next room to be out of my way. I'd call him for his walk and, like the man I'd met in the pine forest with the runaway dog, he wouldn't come. Trezza had to fetch him to the door for me.

In the evening, eating my dinner in front of the television, I looked at him as he turned his face away, and I wished he wasn't there. Could we send him back? No, not least because I'd discovered that Trezza forms a bond with her dog that you wouldn't want to see broken. When she and her ex separated she kept Mingus for the first six months. But Mingus spent all his time waiting by her new front door for his Master to come home. In the end she complied with Mingus's clear wishes and full-time custody was transferred. I noted the sub-plot here: this episode at least illustrated that a dog can form a stronger attachment to one human carer than to another, even when it has a comfortable relationship with both. But the situation we were in was different. I didn't want to use the word, with its whiff of California psychobabble, but all the same it seemed to me that Ollie and I had got ourselves locked into a *dysfunctional* relationship. He was refusing my love, that was the way I saw it.

The Incident of the Smack had been coming. His

demeanour had been deteriorating in the weeks that led up to it: the backing off, the turning his face, the flinching, the fannying about at the end of the walk. And, to make it worse, as far as I could remember, there was no specific point of origination for it. I couldn't even identify how this had all started, apart from those night-time empty outs in the beginning. Was that really enough to bring us to this: Trezza's equilibrium thoroughly disturbed, me in a black mood as a dog ever so gingerly conceded to take sirloin steak from my hand? What sort of animal remains undelighted to be fed organic beef by his Master? Would I have sent him back if I lived on my own?

I think I would. I think I'd have justified it by saying that dogs and I are not cut out for each other, that I had done my best but that it hadn't worked out. It would have been no surprise. One or two of my friends hadn't bothered to disguise their honest reaction to the news of his arrival.

'You? A *dog!?*'

The way it was said, it flagged something else. The idea that Ollie was a child substitute wasn't even worth arguing with – Trezza has no children, we've been together a few years, it's amateur psychology successfully applied. But there was more to it than that. I'm urban (Norwich has a received image, but I do live on the *Eastside*), I have urban interests. I play football, and after that I go out for a drink wearing my nice clothes that do not get messed up and are not host to dog hairs and residual dog drool. Ollie was a signal of a personality change, an indicator of the mid-life crisis: 'You'll be moving to the country next.' This was the implication. Someone sneeringly mentioned a barn conversion. So, even as an idea, Ollie jarred. And the reality, as it turned out, was not that I had acquired an incongruous pet (noun: *a domesticated or tamed animal or bird kept for companionship or pleasure and treated with care and affection*), rather that I had acquired a massive problem that pissed and shat in the house and which I could not deal with. So maybe the friends had been right. But on the other hand, Trezza's bond aside, I have the usual male complaint: I don't like to be beaten. The sort of writer I am is the kind Thomas Mann identified: somebody for whom writing is more difficult than it is for other people. And so it follows that the variety of not-being-beaten I go in for tends to involve activities that I struggle with in the first place.

I scanned the Yellow Pages and found a classification

called 'Dog Training' (yes, we still needed to get round to that) which had a re-direction to a section called 'Animal Behaviourists'.

Trezza made the call. She described Ollie's primary symptom: takes fright upon sight of Master. An arrangement was made for the man from 'Happy Pets' to come and observe us. Observe was not a word I liked the sound of. The man was called Attila. I shook my head. It was becoming a farce. If there's one cultural device I hate more than a musical it's a farce – a forced construction of ludicrously improbable events that are supposed to be funny, but aren't.

Still, I entered into the spirit of the wretched thing. I walked around whistling the theme from The Dambusters and trying to remember not to mention the war. Attila was a man's name, at least there was that: very few males who visited the house received anything in the way of a welcome from Ollie. Plumbers, paper boys, meter readers, friends: all more or less scary, all to be shied away from. At least Attila would see it like it was. It would have skewed the observation if the observer had been a woman. Ollie prefers women, sometimes he even startles us all by wagging his tail at one. The rescue centre staff had all been female, and aside from their sympathetic dispositions each of them had pockets full of treats, which I noticed they handed out freely. Ollie's first contact with friendly humans had been gender-biased, no question. His experiences at Snetterton were key, I was sure of it. Add to this his early painful separation from his mother, and the complexity of his Oedipal crisis becomes clear.

I can put it like this, in hindsight, as if it were a joke. At the time I was feeling sick, hyper-ventilating; sometimes I didn't even want to enter my own home, where, inside, a skinny animal was dictating the atmosphere. What sort of madness *was* this? And I was as keen to have a animal psychologist come round – and to pay money for it – as I'd have been to visit a quack on my own account. Where I come from we don't do shrinks, where I come from you have a hard life and you get on with it, you kick the dog on your way in from work, not just to keep him in his place, but to make you feel better, too. (This may be myth, ergo it contains the grain of truth.)

Attila was a kindly looking man, originally from the former Czechoslovakia. He came into the house in a quiet, unobtrusive way and watched Ollie from the corner of his eye as he stood and asked us questions. We ran him through the situation. He rolled nuggets of dry food across the floor towards Ollie. Ollie would step from his basket to pick up the food ever so cautiously, then retreat. Attila had a little clicker in his hand which he said could be helpful: click it every time he gets the food, and this he will come to understand as a signal of a good thing. Click, food, click, food.

'Food is a dog's primary motivation,' he said. Make food fun, hide it, throw it for him to find, it can be a game. A dog in the wild will go for a week without eating, then raid a dustbin, then go another few days, catch a rabbit, finish that off, and so on. They don't have meal times, like us; we impose such a routine upon them.

'Ah ha', we said, wondering exactly how this would help with Ollie's fucked up mind.

Attila addressed me directly. 'Only you,' he said, 'Must feed him. Not Trezza. If you become his sole supply of food, he will have to come to you. Use the clicker,' he said, 'Because he may already have bad associations connected to the sound of your voice. It might remind him of another person's voice, a

114

person who was unkind to him, as well as the negative associations he has already formed.'

I'd confessed about the smack. Attila didn't seem to think it was too much of a crime. He was certain that a dog ought to be able to get over such a thing. 'Buy a whistle for calling him when you're outdoors,' he said. 'Train him with food treats first, indoors, so he will associate the whistle with food, too: it will help control him. In time, he will develop trust in you.'

'But why has he become frightened in the first place?' I asked, 'I mean, he was more or less okay at the beginning.'

'Who knows?' Attila said, 'Rescue dogs can be strange, you can only guess what they have been through. The thing to do is to correct the behaviour, and food is the key.'

So. This seemed simple enough. There was no hypnotism or acupuncture, no gizmos, no couch. All that had been laid out was a plausible assessment of canine motivation, a new regime recommended, and a clicker supplied.

Trezza mentioned that Ollie was not so friendly in the specific sense that he seldom wagged his tail.

'We can teach that,' Attila said, 'if you want.' He

clicked the clicker a few more times in a rhythm. 'Once trust has been established, the clicker can be used for more advanced commands. It's how you get dolphins to jump out of the pool for the fish,' he said. 'They hear it click once, they jump to a certain height for the reward. They hear it click twice, it's a better reward, they jump higher. And so on.'

All this was news to me. I wasn't entirely happy with it, either. We were talking circus now – more elevated than a farce maybe, but only about par with a musical. I also found something sinister in the suggestion of wag-training; it would be like teaching an unhappy child to smile to order.

I asked Attila what else he did with dogs, to deflect the conversation away from Ollie's tail, to relax into generalities. He ran socialisation classes, he said. Ah yes, we had plans to get round to those, once Ollie was fit to take along, as it were. Not much chance of us starting group therapy while it was still a possibility he might piss himself at the sight of me.

'And agility,' he said.

Jumping over hurdles and so on, I'd seen that once. It looked good, an element of the steeplechase.

'And dancing,' he said.

I'd seen that too, on Crufts, where ladies in jog pants spin ribbons on sticks and shake their booty alongside Fifi. This was the moment to thank Attila and show him out. Whatever our problems, I felt it safe to say they would never involve Ollie and I hiring tuxedos and performing a tango.

***

If Attila's advice was quite straightforward, Ollie didn't hear it. I became his sole feeder, and he would consume his meal, eventually, but only after I'd left the room, because eating, like shitting, was ideally a private activity for him. He always (still) shoots glances over his shoulders as he bolts his mouthfuls as fast as he possibly can. Nothing bad ever happens at mealtimes, no one ever comes to steal his food from him, but his method never changes. It's a legacy of the forest that he simply cannot shake. We'd forgotten to mention this characteristic to Attila. When Ollie first came home his eating rate was so fast that we were worried and questioned the vet about it. The vet asked us to time him. It took him under a minute to consume a regular portion, a speed the vet described as 'technically, starvation-rate'.

We gave him regular, smaller dishes in the hope that he'd slow down a bit, but there was only so much food he could get into himself in a day, otherwise it came out of both ends. So even as we were embarked on the feed-bonding programme, his stomach was an unsettled area. Anything can start him off. I once made the mistake of giving him a bone from a leg of lamb which precipitated weeks of diarrhoea (in between his regular loads).

As time went on, I became obsessed with the quality of his turds, and in this I am not alone. Watch dog-walkers: the animal stoops, craps, clears the area. Depending on where, when, and type of owner, this may be followed by the picking-up. But say we're in a copse (all owners leave it behind in a copse) – observe the pause and the slight lean forward as an inspection is made for consistency, shape, colour, quality and quantity. Excrement, for the dog owner, is as the tealeaf to the clairvoyant – a rule-of-thumb barometer to health, fortune and well-being.

I have a friend from the north, Peter Kadic, a Ridgeback owner, who is the antidote to the friends who thought I was a weirdo for getting a dog. Kadic is a committed dog-lover, a man who took his beloved Bruce to be cremated when he passed away, and insisted on going to watch because he didn't want the crematorium people, 'Fobbing me off wi' t' bones of any old Fido.'

Kadic phones me much more often since Ollie arrived because Ollie was the signal that I had finally become a proper (northern) man. And of course, I was now equipped to talk the dog talk. As we were talking shit on one occasion, Kadic came up with the perfect definition for the ideal in stools. 'Foster', he said, 'You want to be able to trip over 'em, not slide in 'em.'

Incidentally, Ollie clears the crapping area very fast indeed – he generally celebrates the deposit with a 50 metre sprint of joy. I've heard it said that if you ever see a greyhound take a dump before a race, it's a good bet; I'd say that was sound advice.

His eating rate did slow down a little during this time, but that was about it so far as any improvement went. Between meals I hand-fed him warm chicken and all the rest of his favourites, which he'd take timorously, in a tremble, as if it might be poison – his eyes crazed and fearful. He repeatedly looked to his mum. What had he done to upset her? Why wasn't she looking after him?

I wondered about this program. I could see how it could fail disastrously: he might develop a secondary fear to go alongside the one he'd already got, he might become afraid of Trezza, too.

***

There was the other problem to deal with, the not coming back. Attila had suggested that I recall him and put him on the lead at odd points during the walk – using the clicker or the whistle – when he wouldn't expect it, so he'd get used to my handling and come to accept it. We began an experimental period whereby the three of us went out walking together – I needed Trezza with me for back up. At the odd points it worked, after a fashion. I used Cheddar and the whistle; there was something creepy about the clicker that I did not like. Though Ollie was still as wary as a lamb, had to be whistled many times, flirted away, and remained wholly distrustful, he would, finally, and with a flinch, allow me to take hold of him. If this didn't look too promising, it wasn't: at the end of the walk there was no improvement at all.

Trezza stood by as he flitted about. Yes, it was all very frustrating, she could see that, but it was no reason to send him back to the kennels, was it, opening the way for who knows what kind of evil deviant to pick him up, take him away, and batter and mistreat him, the poor little mite.

Had I even mentioned returning him?

'Yes, last week.'

After about fifteen minutes of driving me insane, Trezza shouted at him and he sat down and allowed himself to be taken hold of – by her – the poor little mite. *I* was supposed to use a whistle to call him in case my voice frightened him, but Trezza only had to give him the old fishwife treatment to make him behave. There had been a couple of moments in my life when I'd been more hacked off than this but on those occasions I'd told the boss to go fuck himself and collected my cards. This was not an option I had in this instance.

***

Though it was happening in minute and reversible increments, invisible to the naked eye – and no casual

observer would think we were getting anywhere —
there *were* some days that were better than others.
With just the two of us out walking again (it had
to be done), I began to put the whistle-training
we'd been practising at home into the service of
calling him off some of his friends among the rest
of the world's dog population.

The whistle was a slim, silver, specialist instrument
purchased from a 'country man' shop with a finely-
calibrated thread in order that it could be set to
different pitches for different commands (ha
ha — for use with Border collie-crosses only). I wore it
on a silver chain round my neck, which, besides
introducing the note of bling, made me feel more of a
professional. By now I had noted that certain other
owners were giving Ollie a very wide berth, and not
without cause. The time had come for me to demonstrate my guru methodologies in public. Instead of
hiding behind trees I could walk along tooting. After a
while, Ollie got the hang of this. He would raise his
head, look around, glance my way.

'Who, me? You're kidding aren't you?' the glance
said.

He'd carry on with his game — taunting his friend,

Perkins the Jack Russell, with his superior speed before flipping him on his nose like a seal with a ball, going fifteen rounds with some far-away border terrier — until he was done. As he finally came back to a distance that I could vaguely regard as being within my orbit, I'd give an extra long blast.

'Good boy,' I'd say, 'Well done.'

That showed them.

***

The most tolerant of other owners were the other rescuers, and most specifically the rescue-lurcher owners, who were a help. Though Ollie was an extreme example, they understood what it was like, and their own dogs gave very good chase. Some lurcher owners claimed that their animals were pretty smart, but others were more honest and stated the obvious — one of the problems with them is that, in many cases, they don't have too much going on between their ears. This reinforced the view that I'd been coming to, namely that Ollie was quite a stupid animal, what with his general untrainability (he was *still* not clean in the house at night time), his multiple warinesses, and his inability to get beyond 'Sit' so far as a command was concerned.

All the same, he was certainly smart enough to second-guess me when it came to the end of playtime. In the absence of Trezza, his backsliding was impressive. He could sense the turning point in a walk whatever route I took; as soon as we entered the second half I could see his guard go up and his distance increase. I would have made my life a lot easier by never ever letting him off the lead, of course, but since I'd identified that his vocation (running) was also his principal joy in life, I couldn't do that to him. I'd vary entry points, parking north, south, east and west of the campus in order to confuse him, which would work for a short while, say, day one. But as soon as he was familiar with the route, say, day two, the recall situation began to recur.

***

As a break from the university-walk stress, I'd sometimes drive to the Norfolk coast which, at the nearest point, is only twenty miles away. He didn't know where he was when we got there, a disorientation that helped. At the beach he could indulge in a major workout – he adored the sand which contained great hidden treasures like seagull guano, and dead fish. Most days at the university he rolls in fox shit. The shit of the fox has a musky, unpleasant smell, though I prefer it to that of the seagull; out here he found a decomposing fish to roll in, which was the worst smell yet, until he found the dream combination of a decomposing fish that a seagull had shat on, a combination of aromas to make a grown man retch. The received wisdom is that the instinct which impels them to engage in this repellent activity is 'scent-masking,' to disguise their own aroma when they're on the hunt. My own view, based on the observation that Ollie has never caught a rabbit, or anything else, is that he does it because he likes it.

Shay, the Galway City taxi driver, explained to me that he never would catch a rabbit either, by the way. This was because I had made some fundamental errors of omission in his early life. At about six months you need to coach your lurcher in the art of stealth, see: the animal doesn't have it naturally. How you do it is you edge him in close to the prey, quiet like, along the bushes, restraining him on a cord held tight through the ring of his collar. As you get to within a few feet of the rabbit he will be pulling hard, straining at the leash, desperate. Now you give a little signal, let go, and Wallop! He's got his boy and there you have it: four lucky feet, one lucky tail and a meal ready for the pot. Without this tuition the dog will always go too early, alerting the prey, allowing the window of opportunity for it to escape.

By the time I knew about all this, of course, it was too late. So far as Ollie is concerned, rabbits puzzle him. Sometimes he gets close to an especially young or dense one, stops, and watches in incomprehension as it shuffles sideways towards its warren pretending to be invisible. *What* is its problem? Why won't it come and play? He continues to chase them through the dunes, hoping one day to come across a sociable example.

Once he's finished with that, the beach affords much more in the way of getting down with his bad self: digging to Australia, eating seagull feathers, seaweed and live crabs, hurdling the groynes, sliding in the sand, jumping back from the scary waves, and conducting long staring matches with the seals that bob out of the shallows. He still shows zero inclination to return to me, but all this activity is tiring and works up an enormous appetite. His stomach lures him in. Eventually.

Sighting one of those shy rabbits

The wild dunes behind the beach out at Winterton, a bleak, beautiful stretch a few miles to the north of Yarmouth – deserted most of the year, with the exception of dog walkers – was our favourite spot. Even here I'd come across people taking their animals for walks on leads. More often than not I'd have to make my way over to them, to field Ollie out of their way.

I'd look at them curiously. They'd sometimes

respond to the curious look, typically claiming one of two stories: either their dog was 'a bit funny', a euphemism for 'attacks other animals', or else it had once been attacked itself, most often when it was young, and since then it had always been withdrawn and nervy. Whichever type of leash-bound dog they had, here they were, a part of that weird brand of person, the dog owner, out in all foul weathers, evidently devoted to the animal in question and just as evidently unhappy, trapped in mutual dependency at either end of a three-foot strap.

I noticed that some of these people looked at me as if I were lucky, having a dog that could be trusted to roam free, that didn't attack others, that would come back, that seemed, on the face of things, quite content – boisterous, assured, just a little bit scatty. 'If only you could see him at home,' I said, 'You wouldn't believe it.' I'd trot out my new catch phrase: Jekyll and Hyde.

I began to feel sorry for dog owners. If I hadn't been so consumed by trying to resolve our relationship I might better have been able to see how like them I was becoming, and I could have spent a moment feeling sorry for myself, or at least attempt a dispassionate assessment of my condition: by now, in devoting myself to getting Ollie to function as an acceptable pet, I was losing three to four hours a day.

It's difficult to make a case for this, but I managed it. One of the old truisms of writing is that most of it consists of waiting, waiting for the muse to strike and so on. I latched onto this conceit and I held it dear; I could at least look at all these hours as time I'd only be spending doing nothing anyway, as a normal part of the job description.

At the conclusion of beach walks, in the back of the knackered estate, I'd feed and water Ollie, and after he was done I'd give him a couple of extra treats and tickle him under the chin. Even as spent as he was, torso relaxed, dead on his feet, he'd still back off and look at me as if to say, 'Please don't do that.'

***

On our return home, as I'd mentioned to the beach walkers, it was a different dog that skulked into the house. He had quickly recognised that he only received his food from me: he's very swift to understand a pattern – in fact, once he's established a routine, he's extremely loathe to deviate from it. Trezza describes him as autistic, and his behaviour is consistent with the particular strand of autism whereby if a certain activity doesn't happen in the same way and at the same time every day – the first walk, the first poo, the first meal; the second walk, the second poo, the second meal – it freaks him all the more. You can trace the tension in his muscles as he fidgets neurotically like a tiger in a zoo, waiting, waiting. He hardly ever barks (because barking scares him and makes him run away from himself); his responses are mostly mute, physical. (On those rare occasions when he does give voice we can be sure something serious is occurring; he is being rounded on by three other dogs at once, he is cornered and is about to lose a battle.)

Still, he didn't come forward for his meal, like Mingus or any other dog I've ever met. He hid while he waited for it to happen to him, while he waited to be called. Only then might he peep round the corner of the door which leads from the dining-room into the hall. I would be at the other end of the corridor, in the kitchen, with the bowl of dry food and a tin of pilchards. He could not bridge this gap — twelve feet — without assistance. I had to lay a trail of chicken pieces to enable him to make the journey. Once he'd made it, he'd crouch trembling by his bowl as he ate. Then, suddenly, he'd jump. What now? I'd look round to see that the apron had inadvertently been left hanging on the kitchen door. Only once it was removed could he bring himself to finish his bowl.

I thought about myself and the apron in terms of a nasty man, the monster in Ollie's mind for whom I was such a great substitute. Ollie had been collected from the wild at about two months. Say he'd been wandering for one week before being rescued. Or let's push it and say maybe two weeks, at the outside. That would allow a mere six or seven weeks prior to that for a man to have been nasty and left an over-whelming impression. It's not *that* long, but clearly it's long enough. As Ollie slunk away after his dinner, without a backwards glance, I grew to despise and resent the nasty man myself.

The days and weeks passed and nothing changed. Sometimes I'd visit a house with a normal dog in it — a dog who welcomed humans with barking and jumping up and licking. This only served to illustrate how much Ollie differed to a domesticated pet. He seemed unable to de-program himself from the notion that I was his depraved warder, who might, at any time, turn on him and beat him to a pulp. In order to try better to understand him, I began logging on to various Saluki websites. (Experienced lurcher owners always greet me with the line, 'That's a nice Saluki-greyhound you've got there' – there's not much cross, it's the Saluki in him that is dominant.) Online I learned that Salukis have a very unusual characteristic. Believe it or not, if you tick them off, these animals can actually hold a grudge for an hour or two. If only.

***

It's a favourite trope of wildlife programmes to demonstrate how animals deploy their strategies, talents, and saving graces in the service of their own personal survival.

Ollie was growing ever more stunning to look at. Here, at least, was his saving grace. After several changes of feed (and numerous consultations with the vet which involved, for an unsuccessful stint, a vegetarian diet, following some chronic fits of indoor, and *in-car*, diarrhoea) his coat had developed a brilliant sheen; he gleamed like an otter, and was fitter than a flea.

His movement was becoming superb. Much as he was decimating my timetable, and making my life difficult, he was capable of stopping the traffic with his running and leaping; like a hare at full tilt, he could even change direction in mid-air. I'd sometimes turn from admiring this to see that I was part of a larger audience, smiling and nodding in quiet appreciation. Here was his saving grace and his talent rolled into one, and the talent he put to good use. He developed particular relationships with dogs that he met regularly.

He knew to avoid certain cases, Sparky, for example, a mean, heavyweight, elderly and irascible Belgian Shepherd, who had nipped Ollie on his backside once as a way of telling him where he could stick his jaws-wide-open neck-sledging routine. Ollie never forgot the nip and took to hurdling Sparky whenever their paths crossed, and he did the same with any other Belgian Shepherd, too, just in case.

Sparky's owner was equally irascible. Held

together by bits of string, he was an old boy who was the first living person I've ever seen carrying a crook. I never saw him beat Sparky with the crook, but he'd jab him with it, and he shouted at and bollocked the dog most of the time, for all it was worth — it never made a scrap of difference.

Sparky seemed perfectly happy to take an earful and the odd prod as the trade-off for doing more or less as he liked. I began to wonder if some dogs were simply unbiddable, that they got on with their thing whatever you tried and that was that.

Milla was another.

MILLA

We came across Milla some time after our darkest days. Milla is a Dobermann rescued from
the streets of London, then named after the
Cameroonian footballer Roger Milla, who celebrated
the goals he scored at Italia '90 by doing the Makossa
– the rhythmic step-forward dance – around the corner flag. An odd name for a dog, you might think,
until, that is, you see Milla (the dog) shaking his booty.

Milla is the opposite of Sparky in the sense that he
is one of Ollie's closest friends. More often than not,
the first I knew of Milla's presence was that, in his

excitement to get to Ollie, he bowled me over by smacking into the back of my knees. I'd look behind as I got onto my feet. Where was Milla's master? (Like parents at the school gates – 'Oh, hello, are you Naughty Victoria's mum?' – I mainly know the dog's names, not those of the owners.) Milla's master was nowhere in sight: in this respect, at least, Milla's master was like me.

Every time Milla and Ollie met, each jubilant occasion which began with gangsta handshakes and high fives, the two of them would be united by a single ambition: to better the quality of the rumble they'd had the last time. It began with Milla chasing Ollie, in a figure of eight, through a chicane, then a reverse, then a playfight, then picking a playfight with another dog, then picking a playfight with a second dog, and a third, and so on, with time-outs given for group brawling.

Milla's master would finally appear, having been left behind in a copse some way back. Milla would ignore him entirely, choosing instead to dive-bomb my pockets where he knew treats were kept. He must have weighed three times Ollie, and he was a Dobermann. The Dobermann – a blend of Pinscher,

Terrier and Rottweiler as *The Giant Book of the Dog* will tell you – is a breed developed over a century ago by a German tax collector and part-time dog-catcher, a breed designed to protect the taxman whilst he was out dog-catching. In short, a breed developed to be fierce (it makes a terrific family pet, obviously, given firm handling).

In my pre-Ollie days, I would have gone out of my way to avoid a character like Milla, and even now that I knew a little of dogs, I still found him fairly alarming. He has the maddest orange eyes, like shattered marbles. Was Ollie frightened of him? After they'd done with their fighting, or sometimes during it, Ollie would try to hump his friend. As mentioned, Ollie has

Milla comes to say hello

been neutered, but having his equipment decommissioned doesn't stop him from feeling horny, and he makes no distinction between dogs and bitches either. Experienced owners told me he was displaying a form of dominance. (This was where I got my line for the Labrador owner at the outset; this common lore is the way in which the word is passed along.)

Ollie's humping was an activity which appalled Jack, if it happened to take place when he was around. Jack has the characteristic homophobia associated with teenage boys and routinely uses the word 'gay' as a term of abuse.

'That dog's *gay* dad,' he'd say in a suitably horrified tone.

'Bisexual,' I'd reply.

But whatever his preference or orientation, his behaviour out here in the open was not easy to square with his indoor persona. My best guess was that he felt safe engaging in these lurid acts because he knew that if it came to the crunch he could use his talent – his agility, his speed – to remove himself from danger. This could not apply back in the cage of our home.

I watched him rear-ending Milla. Here you had the full Ollie-paradox: frightened of flies, aprons, curtains, his loving owner, yet prepared to attempt anal intercourse with a killer-dog. On occasions I'd seen him try it on with a Great Dane, a Rottweiler and a bull-mastiff, all male, all four times his size.

'Behaving himself, is he?' Milla's owner would say, as he finally caught up referring to his own charge. 'Oh yes, great,' I'd reply. And I meant it. Because Milla was one of the other naughty kids in class, the ones who help cast my own little angel in a better light.

Through the course of their game, which typically sprawled into the biggest available space – the football and rugby pitches – the other dogs that came and went provided more or less of a distraction. Ollie might try his luck, taunt a bonus run out of a distant Labrador, and often he'd get it. He could cross the ground in seconds. The distant owner would invariably be calling their dog on, not keen.

They continued to bemuse me, these people. Early in the morning, the sun out, nature showing off her new blooms, yet the prime pleasure they seemed to take in all of it was to exert authority over an animal who *only wants to play*, to demonstrate a superiority over rogue owners like me and Milla's master – reprobates who introduced dogs into the public domain which were out of control.

Labradors can be very fit, athletic dogs, incidentally and, though it's probably too late to save myself insofar as Labrador owners are concerned, Ollie numbers many friends among this breed, as in turn I have come across many excellent Labrador owners who ARE NOT STIFFS.

***

But before we ever met Milla we were still in our darkest days, and at the conclusion of our walks Ollie persisted with his neurotic evasions.

When at last I got hold of him, or someone else did it for me, I was all too often in a filthy humour, a black mood, blackened further because my options to act were so restricted. I knew that to shout, like Sparky's owner, or to whack him on the nose – or make as if to – as I'd seen others do, would only increase the fear and confusion that was already swimming in his eyes, an expression that remained unchanged even as I gave him his treats in the back of the car, his reward for being good enough to drop his guard so low as to finally allow himself to be caught.

After a particularly grim morning outing, I replayed an especially grim scene from it in my head as I fed Ollie his bits. He had dashed behind the long hedge to sledge some timid puppy, ruining someone's day (I was left in no doubt about this), a someone who probably had to get to work, a someone for whom time was limited and precious, not a cloud-cuckoo-land dweller like me. As I fed him, it dawned on me much more clearly what had been going on with the staff who taught in one of the middle schools that Jack went to. This school had a high number of statemented pupils, children who would receive a team point or a gold star on those happy days when they didn't throw chairs round the classroom or bite a fellow student on the ankle. The catch-all expression used to exonerate the antics of these headbangers was ADS, Attention Deficit Syndrome. I had a problem with the method the school teachers employed to deal with these cases, the system of reward. The problem I had was that it was all the un-statemented children who paid the price as the classroom was cleared while negotiations with the offending individual took place and lessons were lost. It was this politically correct half-witedness that was the principal reason that we took Jack out of that school. I recalled the methods employed by the teachers while Ollie took his last piece of steak, and I had the blinding flash: I could suddenly see how the owners of the normal dogs out in the park might see things. Did Ollie have ADS, I wondered? What *was* this animal's strategy for survival?

Insofar as our relationship was concerned he didn't appear to have one: in fact he seemed to be going backwards. Once I'd found him a few extra mouthfuls of old cheddar from my B-stash of treats, and he had semi-settled on his sheepskin throw in the car, he might relax enough to accept a stroke without fully flinching. This remained the standard; this was as good as it got between us in any confined space.

Back home I experimented with some new tactics aimed at improving relations. I tried ignoring him, but he just ignored me back. I lay flat on the floor to be lower than him, in a passive, submissive position, to see if he'd try to dominate me as he would a bull-mastiff. He'd occasionally glance my way to see if I'd gone yet. I'd try him with a squeaky toy: scary. Everything I attempted spooked him. From his point of view, my not being there was definitely best.

Additionally, and to heap on the irritation, he began to express delight upon catching sight of one of my male friends, Smut, a carpenter. Smut and I used to work together. Smut smells of dog, workshop and sawdust. Aside from these excellent characteristics, his appearance at our house could also be a signal that his own pair of canine companions, Charlie and Louis, might not be far behind (though I didn't think that was the whole reason for Ollie preferring him to me). He would go beyond wagging his tail at the sight of my friend, he would rotate it like a propeller, and even put his feet up on his shoulders and lick him, the treacherous little bastard.

CHARLIE AND LOUIS,
AND OTHER FRIENDS

Like Mingus the Dalmatian, Charlie and Louis have Jazz names, because, like Mingus's owner, their master is a music lover of a certain disposition (one who I've seen practise the trumpet while sitting on the toilet). Inseparable brothers, their generic type is 57 varieties, though Charlie has a pronounced spaniel-ness while Louis is more the pointer. Short and obsessive characters, they are outgoing and friendly, except for Louis, who can be a bit unpredictable in the sense that once in a while he'll take a dislike to another dog and launch an attack. It's not all that funny when it happens, and Smut's partner had a period when she more or less gave up on taking him out for all the aggro he caused. Louis will put up with *any*thing from Ollie, though – ear-chewing, sledging, mounting, growling and more ear-chewing. This is for a particular reason, born of self-interest; the sight of us arriving at their place inevitably signals a bonus walk for him and his brother. We take them down to a nearby meadow with a river passing through it. Charlie and Louis are great swimmers and retrievers of the stick, and they like to combine the two. In an absolutely consistent pattern of behaviour, Louis swims out to

Charlie and Louis

collect the object while his brother paddles idly around the river bank waiting to take it from him and present it back to us. Meanwhile Ollie, who does not swim, stands with his feet in the water and his arse in the air barking a camp 'arf' as he attempts in turn to steal the stick from Charlie, so that he can be the winner of this great game. On the occasions that Charlie deigns to allow Ollie to wrestle the stick, Ollie runs off with it into the long grass where he loses it.

We once took them all to the beach where Louis found a long oar washing into shore. He took a distinct liking to the oar and carried it in his jaws all the way back to the carpark a mile away. It was over six-foot long and sodden, but he never dropped it, nor did he break stride; he was a dog on a mission from God. Though he allows the impression to be formed that it is his brother who is the brains of the team ('Look at this chump,' Charlie seems to say, as he walks the same mile unencumbered, removing the treasure from Louis in the last ten feet, to plant it at your feet, a personal gift), it is Louis who has the idea in the first place, and it is Louis who does the graft.

The incident of the oar confirmed an impression I had already formed; namely, that if I ever undertake an expedition to the North Pole, Louis is the dog I will take with me. When it all goes wrong, Louis will only eat small parts of my carcass, the remainder he will drag back to civilization, where no doubt his brother will be waiting to take the credit for the heroic rescue work. At the funeral Charlie will do a great job of looking mournful with his big mournful eyes, but everyone will know where the real acclaim lies.

After the bonus walk, I take Ollie back to Charlie and Louis's place in order that he can observe the behaviour of normal dogs – both within the doors of a house, and towards me. It is all relaxed, all happy and chilled. Louis lies on a blanket, Charlie jumps up to sit on my knee. Ollie stands outside the back door in a courtyard flitting backwards and forwards, a mad look in his eyes: as with when I cock my leg, he seems to see no relationship between any of this and himself.

***

There was just one sole occasion on which he perked up at my appearance. I came home after he'd had been out with Trezza and another male friend. This friend had accidentally bashed Ollie in the head on the backswing of throwing a big stick (my thoughts went to the Vizsla breeder in Reading when I heard this tale, introducing, as it did, a new variation on the dangers involved).

Ollie looked up at me piteously from under his throw as I came in, like a child in its sick bed. For the first time ever he was after my sympathy. As I sat down beside him on the floor he went so far as to nearly rest his chin in my lap. I tickled behind his ears and he didn't seem to mind. It looked like a breakthrough. Perhaps the bump on the head had done him some good? The following day, though, it was business as usual, his return to type as swift as it was predictable. It was with all seriousness that I considered that a possible route forward would be for me to pay somebody to clock him one every day.

Still, at least he was not pissing himself any more at my approach. Except that one afternoon when I came in through the back door, minding my own business, he caught sight of me and he did it again in the middle of the kitchen floor, a relapse made worse because I could conceive of no for reason it. If I'd have been asked how it was going at this point, immediately before this piss, I would have said the curve was ever so slightly upwards, but this moment stood in contradiction to such an opinion. It was completely retrograde and it upset me a lot.

We were getting nowhere. If I could not walk about my own house without a dog wetting himself, the time had come to seek more help. I leafed through *Why Does My Dog Do That?*, a paperback that a friend had been kind enough to give me, but the writer seemed to be talking about a different manner of creature altogether to Ollie, one that might be capable of making a reasoned connection between A and B. So I phoned Snetterton to see if they had any other psychologists on their books. Attila had provided partial assistance, but I would certainly take a second opinion.

There was an attached vet on duty who spoke to me at length. I can't remember much of the words he said, though the tone I remember with clarity. He talked down to me to such an extent that I took to interjecting (when I could get a word in edgeways) with multi-syllables and stray words from the margins of Cultural Studies – *mythologies, paradigmatically, Roland Barthes* – just to try to throw him. The main thrust of his lengthy sermon was that the few months

I'd had Ollie in my life was a very short time indeed, that surely I ought to be able to find it within myself, as a rational adult, to remain patient. He cited cases he knew of that were far, *far* worse. I *could*, he supposed, as a last resort, return the animal, but would this not be a course of action that would cast me into the light of being something of a failure?

For a long while after this 'conversation' I lay on the floor in my office – which is covered in rough seagrass and is painful to lie on – trying to relax by once more using those deep-breathing calming techniques that I'd heard of, the ones that didn't work at the end of our walks. If I wasn't careful, it would only be a matter of time before Ollie drove me to yoga, or some other dubious Eastern practice that would be even less like me than owning a dog.

It's only right to say that this particular vet was the sole rogue representative of his profession that I've encountered. Ollie's many visits to veterinarians (in addition to his psyche, and his delicate stomach, he has become an accident waiting to happen) have otherwise been distinguished by great care and professionalism, though there is one obvious caveat. Here is the one concrete tip I can pass on: if you're going to own a dog, get insurance. Ollie's medical bills topped five thousand pounds before he was even two years old.

On the day following the helpful talk with the NCDL vet, I pulled up on a small dirt carpark from where we were to begin our walk – one of my lesser used 'confusion' start points around the university campus. Ollie leapt out of the back of the car almost before the tailgate was up, as if he'd been planning a breakout. He hurdled a low crush barrier like Steve McQueen launching his Triumph in *The Great Escape*, and landed in the middle of the road, which at that point is on a blind bend. He slid to the opposite pavement where he came to a halt and stood looking back at me. I didn't know whether to call him or tell him to stay. Either option would be equally useless as he'd pay no attention anyway. Predictably, he did the worst thing possible. He came halfway back then stopped on the centre line as he considered his next move. Two cars came from opposite directions and as they crossed, for a split second, he disappeared from my view.

They missed him by the distance of the gap between them. I admit that I was so fed up with him at that moment that I would have considered it a relief if either one of the vehicles or the animal himself had taken a slightly different trajectory. The way he was performing, how much longer could he be for the world anyway? The next motorist slowed right down. Now I called his name and to my surprise he returned and allowed himself to be put on the lead without further trouble: a first.

All the same, I had once more been made to take part in a pantomime involving roads, a dog and traffic. Pantomimes fall below musicals in the cultural Order of Merit. In a reversal of our normal routine I *began* our walk in a foul mood.

***

And so it went on.

I read a story in the paper about the Russian *émigré* artist Marie Marevna, who worked in Paris. She said in an interview that she would have produced more work during her lifetime, but that her dog was always eating her brushes. That helped me.

I took the slightest comfort wherever I could find it. I frequently encountered one lady who roamed the university calling her golden retriever. People would help her out, saying that it had gone this way or that way, that they'd seen it in some bushes back there. I caught sight of the animal a couple of times; it was portly, which was no surprise as it was a walking dustbin whose main purpose in life was to go off for a rummage around the kitchens of all the campus restaurants, scoffing everything in sight, and not to return to its owner until it was full up. She would often be there as we began our walk and still there when we left an hour and a half later.

There was another dog called Linus (named after the Saint, not the character in the Peanuts) who had the habit of going truffle hunting for hours on end, for imaginary truffles. He has very patient owners. Though I have seen them standing about calling his name, to no effect, sometimes in dreadful weather, in winter, when it is dark, and cold, I have never seem them cross or even mildly ruffled. He is a lucky dog.

And there was Max. Max is a border terrier. Border terriers are a breed that were completely under my radar before Ollie. They are comical dogs, as it turns out. Short, ginger, scruffy and tenacious, with a tufty finish like a welcome mat. Border terriers come with endless stamina and attitude, they're the type who both start things and finish them too; if they don't win a scrap outright, they win it on points. And they never give up on a chase – at the outset they may look to have no chance against, say, two greyhounds and a whippet, but, by wearing the other dogs into the ground, they triumph in the end.

Max was a typical example of his breed. His habit in greeting Ollie was to bounce in on his hind legs. By this means his front paws were raised to the ideal height to box Ollie about the face. Like Ali shielding himself from Foreman, Ollie's technique for dealing with this onslaught involved a largely defensive, rope-a-dope repertoire of leaning, fainting and hold-ing-off. He achieved the holding-off by pulling Max from side to side using his ears as levers. This was a game that could go on for twenty minutes.

Meanwhile, Max's owner and I exchanged small talk, content in the knowledge that the wearing-each-other-out that we were watching would be good news for us both in the end. Max was one of the few that could make Ollie submit. This was not good enough for Max, it was not what he wanted, and one way or another he would always provoke Ollie into a second wind, by body-slamming him from a standing start, or by head-butting him from behind. After the second wind was done, with much whistling, offering of treats, and walking away in opposite directions, Max could eventually be persuaded to cease, and we would go our separate ways. And then, having thought about what he was missing, Max would wonder if Ollie had a third wind, and would reappear for more. His owner would show up a few minutes behind and shout while his pet paid him no heed. In a reversal of my normal role, in this sole specific instance, it was *me* who would capture a dog for another owner, an accomplishment which made me love Max, and which enabled me to feel that, even if Ollie wasn't, at least I was coming on a bit.

In the pattern of these things, Max and Ollie saw a lot of each other during one passage of time, and then we got onto different walking shifts and didn't bump into each other for ages. And then, like buses, we met same time, same place, three days in a row. As we extended our small talk, Max's owner told me that since we'd last crossed paths there had been a day when he'd lost his dog completely; Max had shot into the walkways of the accommodation blocks, chasing a rabbit or something, and could not be found. His owner had walked all over the campus calling him for more than two hours before admitting defeat and making his way back to his car. When he got there, Max was sitting waiting by the passenger door as if to say, 'About time, too. Where do you think you've been?'

While Max's disciplinary record gave me no particular hope about how the future might play out, he did supply a crumb of comfort in the moment: he was no better behaved than Ollie; in fact, given that he was a five-year-old who should know better, you could argue that he was worse. In short, I knew of one or two dogs who might possibly have been as exasperating as my own, though it seemed quite clear to me that none of these were actually afraid of their owners. (To double check this, I asked: they weren't.)

WALKING HOME

Ollie's first summer was of the type we get only once in a while in England, the kind in which a heatwave arrives which blisters the tarmac and buckles the rail tracks.

On one of the hottest of all these exceptional days I took him for a walk just before Sunday lunchtime. Why I mistimed this so badly, I don't know; the thermometer was heading up to 100° F, and there I was out with a mad dog in the midday sun. The only slight intelligence I'd brought to bear was that we set off in the shade, using a river path overhung by trees.

The river ultimately meets the broad at the university (by now I knew every single approach to the campus, in addition to different complex internal patterns that you could make within the walk itself).

At a convenient point, Ollie leant forward as far as he could to take a drink, and fell into the river. He refuses to swim – lurchers tend not to (because, I discovered, they don't have webbed feet, like water-loving breeds) – but he can save himself from drowning and can clamber out well enough. Otherwise this part of our walk was incident-free, albeit sweaty and mosquito-heavy. And then we reached the broad.

Sundays were a difficult day for me at the best of times. In addition to the weekend Labrador stiffs, you encounter the whole compendium of other weekend peril: skateboarders; toddlers who are as skittles to a moving dog; fascist all-terrain pram-pushers competing for lane space with the fascist cyclists; family groups with elderly people in the pastel uniform – magnetic in their attraction to a dirty dog's dirty paw or a wet dog's shake; BMXers; kite flyers (multiple tangling opportunities); skateboards being pulled along by parachutes (multiple tangling opportunities squared); games of football, cricket and rounders; pic-nickers with a rug laid out, and a surplus of joggers. You name it, it's there. And then there are many more dogs than usual too, dogs who are not even Labradors, out for their once-a-week stretch and dump. Nation of dog lovers my arse, nation of fat idle bastards more like. This is the mood Sundays put me in.

On this particular Sunday, we arrived at the broad to find quite a few fishermen as well. I'm not generally keen on fishermen, who all too often seem to have a touch of the mass murder about them: loners obsessed with hooks and knives and twine. In turn, they are not generally keen on Ollie, who has a penchant for raiding their maggots. Fishermen are often aggressive in their attitude, territorial. They own the place, don't they? No one must lark about, or swim, or row a boat, no one must disturb the water – it is their crucial activity that takes precedence over all else. Fishermen tend to see Ollie off in short order, without any intervention required from his Master. They are stationed lower than I am, down by the water's edge, and typically hidden behind umbrellas – I hear their oaths, sometimes I catch their dirty looks, but I am already off on my way, quick, in order to avoid any discussions about dog control, discussions in which I would not have a leg to stand on.

Ollie went down to annoy the first of the fishermen. I called him and he turned the deaf ear. He stayed in there and, even by his own poor standards he was overly persistent. An unacceptably long time elapsed while he remained, leaping from one side to the other of the small inlet in which the fisherman was stationed. This forced me to intervene, to field him out of the way. As I attempted to act he flew into the fisherman's equipment, scattering it. The fisherman cursed and I did not blame him. It was beyond the pale for me not to pretend some sort of authority, so I overturned a ground rule and I shouted at Ollie. This *did* have the effect of clearing him. I apologised to the first fisherman. Ollie repeated his performance with the second fisherman. I tried to get hold of him, to more hopeless avail. He shot on to the third fisherman.

I surveyed the area for a moment. There are low decking platforms at frequent intervals around the lake, platforms which are built for the purpose of fishing from; every single one was occupied, as well as much of the intervening bank. There must have been a hundred rods. I had never seen this taking place before, but it was apparent that what we had here was a fishing contest. I may not care for fishermen, I may find the idea of a fishing challenge in an artificially stocked lake faintly absurd, but all the same I fully appreciated that these men were engaged in the serious business of sporting competition.

Sporting competition is an activity in which I partake – as participant, spectator and punter – many times a week; sporting competition is a human endeavour of which I am wholly in favour; sporting competition is the antithesis of pantomime. It was my clear responsibility to protect the fishermen's rights not to have a stupid animal jeopardising their chances. Ollie returned to the first fisherman. The first fisherman had had enough and asked me if I couldn't control my fucking dog, for fuck's sake. It was over 100 degrees now, I had been put into three embarrassing positions in a row, I'd been chasing the stupid animal, I was perspiring profusely, and the answer to this question was a negative, though I did not give it. I shouted at Ollie again, even though I couldn't actually see him. He emerged being chased by another fisherman who was brandishing a keep-net at him.

Even taking into account my normal problems in respect of returning him to the lead, there would be absolutely no chance of catching him now since he had been provoked into a state of panic by a combination of brandishing and shouting. So I chased him off down the path, which I knew would do no long-term good, quite the reverse, but I had to do *some*thing to restrict his chances of infuriating all the other competitors. Even in mid-pursuit, he still had a go at a couple more, though by now they were prepared, and were waving tripods and poles at him, practically walkie-talking each other and putting out an APB.

I rounded Ollie into the clearing at the end of the broad. I paused, collected myself, mopped my face with my shirt, and began to offer him the cubes of cheddar that were oozing in my pocket. He backed off, his spine arched, his tail between his legs touching his chest, his ears flat to his head.

To all the assembled Sunday Labrador walkers et al, I must have looked like the local dog-batterer. I offered him the cheese again. He ran away over the footbridge. On the other side of the bridge lay the pitches, where further sporting contests were taking place. I'd had enough. I mentally declined the prospect of chasing him across a cricket wicket. I was steaming.

'I'll abandon the little shit,' I thought. 'Why not? I'll tell Trezza he ran away and I couldn't find him.'

I doused my face in water from the river and turned. I pulled down my shades so I could pass by all the fishermen incognito, and I retraced my steps on my way back to a normal life. I felt like lighting a cigar. Halfway down the broad I took a right into the shady path beside the river. I never looked back.

Some way along the path, about three-quarters of a mile from where I'd last seen Ollie, a stretch of decking had been laid down to compensate for a patch of swampy ground. As I walked across it I heard the scratch of claws behind me. I turned. His body language was unimproved since I'd last seen him, to the extent that he was actually managing to walk with his back up and his tail between his legs. He took two more steps, then stopped and trembled.

I looked him in the eyes. I made an interpretation of the expression I saw there. It was a complex message which said, 'Listen, we can't go on like this. I want us to be friends, but I don't know how we can do that because I am petrified of you.'

I paused, then I crouched. He sat, continued to

tremble, but didn't move. We stayed there like that for a long time until eventually I put him onto the lead.

There were many more vastly irritating days ahead, but as we faced each other while we melted under the midday sun, on the decking over the swampy ground, we had turned some sort of corner.

***

Tale-of-woe rescuers aside, there were frequent occasions when other dog owners, who'd had a rescue in the past, whose minds may have been clouded by time, would offer their thoughts. 'From the home, you say? They're the best, they're so true and faithful; they never forget what you've done for them.'

These words were another way of saying the old truism: Man's best friend.

In making the effort to find me after I had abandoned him, Ollie had demonstrated how this sentimental tosh actually works. Discovering himself alone, he'd marshalled the crude and admirable urge for survival. He has the saving grace of beauty, talent in abundance, but like all too many humans, he has no strategy to go alongside any of this. If he is autistic, then this is its manifestation: he relies only on instinct. Act first, think later. It's a common complaint, a common autism, and one that I share. I came to writing the long way round, through many rash misjudgements that bypassed anything you might call a thought process. And even my instinct is dodgy – as I've already said, I am Mann's sort of writer, the kind who finds writing more difficult than other people (it normally takes me five drafts before I'll even send a postcard). I thought about this syndrome in terms of Ollie and I came to a conclusion. Ollie, I think, is the sort of dog who finds being a pet more difficult than other dogs.

There was never a worse day than the day of the fishing competition. As we worked our way forward I thought about the famous Groucho Marx one-liner, a take on the old truism: 'Outside of a dog, a book is man's best friend; inside of a dog, it's too dark to read.' I came to think of this less as a joke and more of a perceptive comment about the canine soul.

It was still many months before we settled into anything like a normal relationship. How we negotiated our path in the weeks that followed the fishing competition, the methods we used, I really can't relate, because I don't know what they were. Patience is the only technique I can pass on. The moment we spent crouching and looking at each other by the river stood as a watershed for all of our time together up until that point; it had been harrowing, and the immediate aftermath was post-traumatic for us both. As a matter of self preservation, as a method of healing,

The sort of dog who finds being a pet more difficult than other dogs

your mind often goes fallow in these periods, and I guess that's what happened to us.

We managed to break our cycle little by little, day by day, and all the other mantras associated with modifying destructive behaviour. But, like a pair of lovers giving it one more try, we had no tactics. We had a little hope now, that was all. If I could say anything, I'd say that we began to build a fragile confidence by determining that we preferred not to fail; we are both boys, after all — we don't like to be beaten at things whether we're good at them or not. The one tangible decision I made, if you can call it that, was to give up entirely on the notion of apportioning time in a pre-dog, normal-life manner. I guess I dedicated myself to 'Project Ollie'.

I recall long evenings in the summer when we'd be out late enough to see the sky drift to purple as the light slipped away. I'd talk to the shift workers and the poachers and the itinerants who hang around out of hours, I'd share a sip of their beer while Ollie ran himself ragged with their dogs. I remember on the longest day of the year we arrived back after dark. So as a consequence of the volume of time we were sharing together, we got used to each other better and, while we were at it, Ollie found his exhaustion point, which made him easier to handle. I found I had less trouble getting him to return to me when he was lying down, panting, wasted, and wanting to be carried home.

The nights drew in and the clocks went back, and for the first time this had a practical effect on me. You can let some dogs roam in the dark, but Ollie isn't one of them. The gap between our first and second walk in the short winter days was so brief that sometimes we'd be out and about for most of the daylight hours. And, as bit by bit our confidence together grew, and experience began to show that (albeit eventually) he could be relied upon to return even when he wasn't exhausted, I began to be able to use the time to think. This, I could vaguely regard as work. I had not been able to think while we were out together before because so much of the time had been typified by crisis, and crisis does not allow for thinking, crisis is panic, and panic prevents thought. This I know well, because I began to suffer panic attacks some years ago; I've had them on and off for the biggest part of a decade.

At first I ignored them, like you do with intermittent toothache, hoping they'd go away. And when they didn't go away, and became more frequent, and started happening in weird places where there was no danger or stress or anything you could use to explain them – say, paying in a cheque at a bank counter – I tried some conventional medicine.

I went to the doc, my blood and urine was sampled, I was referred here and there, but all to no avail. I was offered beta blockers, but I knew they only gave you a heart attack so I never took them. I tried some homeopathic remedies which were as potent as wine gums. My main approach after these treatment failures was to revert to plan A and pretend that nothing was happening, that everything was okay. And much of the time everything *was* okay, the attacks were episodes, moments. But they were long moments when they came along, moments during which my heart would be racing, I couldn't breath properly, and I was sweating even without chasing a dog in 100°f. In fact it could start in a cold room. It's difficult to pretend this isn't happening when, in fact, it is. In the aftermath I would feel spent, unable to think, good only for a lie down in a dark room.

In Ollie's second summer he went through a sequence of injuries that necessitated many visits to the vet, and I began to have these attacks at the surgery. It was during a period in which they had been getting worse anyway. I could more or less guarantee one if anybody started encroaching into my personal space and messing about with me, say, at the dentist or the opticians. Something about proximity to other people, while at the same time being out of control, of lacking authority, brought it on. And so, without going

The unlikely rescuer

into detail of the therapy involved – because it's not pertinent to this story, and because I'm superstitious that talking about it will reverse the good it has done – I forced myself to get some alternative help, which – and here I touch the wood – has worked pretty well: I'm about ninety per cent better than I was.

That humans use dogs as a psychological crutch is not in doubt; I see people talking with them every single day. Owners often describe how their animal can sense their distress if they are upset, how they will move to comfort them, or put on a happy face if they are feeling low. It's never been this way for me and Ollie (though I *do* conduct conversations with him). If anything, dysfunctional as it's been, it's *me* who is *his* emotional support. And of course, I look after his physical well-being. The vets business was the final straw for me: I could put up with a certain amount of disruption to my own life as a result of these attacks, but I could not accept a situation whereby I could not take my dog to a surgery — for *him* to be cured for fuck's sake — without me suffering a crisis and people having to worry on my account instead of about the real problem, the gash in his front pad. The way I see it, it was Ollie who finally forced me to the therapy from which I had so long shied away (my attitude to the visit of Attila says it all). In this sense, it was Ollie who rescued me.

***

One morning as we were beginning our walk I met an old boy who had lost his dog, a Staffordshire bull terrier. The animal had been missing for an hour or so, which, by all accounts, was uncharacteristic. In my experience, Norfolk males are amongst the most reluctant in England when it comes to showing emotion; all the same I could see that the man was in misery.

'What's he look like?' I asked.

'Big,' he replied. (This is a typical exchange of information with a Norfolk man.) I said I'd keep an eye out for the animal, but without any hope that I'd find him, which I didn't. By the time we got back to the car, and I was opening the tailgate to let Ollie in, I had forgotten about the lost dog. It took a second glance to notice that the creature sauntering in my direction up the middle of the road was a Staffie, a big one, with a red spotted hankie knotted round his neck (it would have been worth a mention, in the description, the red hankie, I thought). The only other information I had was that he was of good temperament, so I made my way towards him and I attached him to Ollie's lead. As I turned and walked back to the car, wondering what to do next, I saw Ollie staring out of the window and looking cross. He had his head tilted to one side as if to say, 'Oi! What's all this?'

The lost dog had a phone number on its tag. I called it – a mobile – and arranged to meet round the other side of the park. I put the animal in the passenger seat, to prevent a disturbance going on in the back. Ollie glowered at me through the rear-view mirror. 'I've never been allowed to sit there,' the look said. 'What's the game?'

After owner and pet had been reunited, and I had the tenner reward forced on me, I opened the tailgate so the old boy could have a better look at Ollie. To show his proprietorship, Ollie made as if to lick my hand, a first.

The old boy drove off in his car, a MkI Ford Granada with doors in different colours. I notice cars – I noticed that model because it reminded me of the car some hoodlum friends knocked about in when I was young, and even more so of the opening titles to the Seventies cop show *The Sweeney*, of which I was a devotee. There was a time I used to covet a Ford Granada (the 3-litre was 'an absolute torque monster', as one of the hoodlum friends put it) but the moment passed. You don't get many of them about these days – the last time I'd seen one it was up on blocks at a boarding kennels and had a bull-mastiff living in it.

In the very worst of Ollie's early days we booked a last-minute holiday to Greece. We needed a break –

not just from him, but he was part of it. In the same last-minute spirit, we'd had to take such kennelling as was available at short notice. The woman sounded fine on the phone, but when we got there we didn't like her, or her attitude. She was careless, offhand, maybe not entirely sober, and the Ford and its resident did not seem a good sign either. But we were catching a plane out of Stansted in two hours' time – it was either leave him there or forfeit a holiday. As we drove to the airport Trezza fretted and cursed herself for not personally checking the place in advance. I said to forget it, there'd been no time for checking, that we'd sort out a nicer place for the future (we did), that however five-star a kennel might be, for him it'd still be a kennel, wouldn't it, away from his selection of beds and duvets and throws. 'He'll be fine,' I said. Though I thought it unlikely he'd come to any harm, I didn't entirely believe my own words, I was saying them primarily to calm her down, and at moments through the holiday I entertained piteous thoughts about him and his circumstances.

The flight back from Greece was due to land early in the afternoon, which would have given us time to collect Ollie, but it was delayed. It was a Friday, and the last pick-up time allowed at the kennels was 6 o'clock. By the time we were finally driving out of the carpark I was pushing it to make this deadline. Missing the cut would have condemned Ollie to a further weekend's board because the nasty owner didn't open on a Saturday. It was a typical holiday return, rain coming down in buckets, articulated lorries pulling into the overtaking lane for no reason, an accident on the A11. None of this helped me. If the Sweeney had caught sight of us at any point along this drive I'd have been well-nicked: I U-turned on main carriageways, overtook badly on B-roads, cut corners at junctions, lane-hopped, and sped like a torque monster. I was a menace. All of which enabled us to pull in through the kennel gates at 18.01. The woman glanced at her watch and gave me a look, which I returned with interest as I handed her the folding.

With monsoon conditions continuing, it wasn't possible to tell whether Ollie was pleased to see Trezza or not; he took a soaking simply by making his way from his pen to the car. He leapt in, shook himself, and shivered. At that time he was certainly unmoved to see me, and displayed no sign that I might even be considered an improvement on a rain-lashed kennels run by a drunk and featuring a bull-mastiff living in a Ford Granada. Yet I had risked life and limb to get there, just to save him from a couple more nights in a place where I imagined he would prefer not to be.

You lose your marbles when you've got a dog, that's what happens.

***

Ollie is just over two now and I would not be without him. I worry about how I'll replace him when he dies, and already I know it won't be possible. Where I used to notice a pretty girl walking down the street, these days my attention is as likely to be caught, in the first instance, at least, by the good-looking Pointer that she's walking. Worse than a person who keeps a dog, I have become a dog lover. Sometimes I surf websites imagining a playmate for Ollie. Not breeder sites, from where we could get ourselves a sensible puppy that we could train from the outset, but rescue sites, because now we have come through this, I could repeat the exercise.

In my own world I have become the dog guru I

sometimes pretend to be. And as I have come to know one lurcher, lurchers have become my dog. I am 'in the breed', as they say (even if it is an unclassified breed). I know of the distinctions between the different crosses, I know about 'long dogs' and all manner of lurcher ephemera which a couple of years ago would have interested me as much as knowing what sort of tree a birch is. If someone offered me a lurcher fridge magnet now I would take it, and after accepting it, I would probably even use it.

The thought has crossed my mind that I could rescue a very young dog and take it over to Shay in Galway for some tuition. But then the counter

You lose your marbles when you've got a dog; that's what happens

thought has crossed my mind that to be in the company of an accomplished rabbiter might make Ollie feel inadequate. So, for the moment at least, I think better of it.

There will be another dog one day. It's bound to happen.

But there will never be another Ollie.

He slit the pads on his front paws three times in six months, accidents acquired simply by running and catching his feet on glass or flint, each wound requiring stitches and bandages, each episode laying him off for three weeks. At the sight of Ollie our regular vet, Gerhard, shakes his head and reaches for his suture kit. During his periods of convalescence I have sat on the sofa with him, and our trust together has grown to the extent that, in the absence of his friends Milla, Charlie, Louis and all the rest, he has made do with play-fighting me: I put my hand in his mouth and pull on his lower jaw, we have a tug-of-war.

It is three weeks after the third slit pad has healed that he gets knocked over, the accident I mentioned to the young whippet owner at the beginning. I am not with him at the time, he is out with Trezza. In a completely unpredictable manner – going off the path at a point he'd passed a hundred times before without going off the path — Ollic shot sideways, cleared a ditch, and ran into a car (it seems he had sighted a rabbit). The driver had no chance. Trezza was in pieces afterwards, as was I. Fortunately he has been blessed with more lives than a cat, and he needs them. The impact of the collision threw him back into the ditch, his radius and ulna fractured and punctured through the pelt of his front right leg.

The drive to the vet took place through late-night Christmas shopping traffic, lasted a long time, and was particularly harrowing. He was patched up and put on an emergency drip, which he managed to disconnect at some point in the night. Still, he survived that. As he caught sight of me as we arrived to pick him up in the morning, and even with the leg encased in a thick temporary dressing like a human plastercast, he tried to run towards me. It was heartbreaking, and at the same time the embodiment of the type of thinking that got him into trouble in the first place. We drove to an orthopaedic surgical specialist in North Norfolk where he stayed for the best part a week (though they discharged him early — he didn't like it there, and they were anxious to get rid of him, 'before he did any more damage to himself'). He had a six-inch metal plate and ten screws set into the bone, but, apart from this serious injury, the rest was just cuts and bruises: to run headlong into a BMW and live to tell the tale isn't bad going.

Back home his three month rehabilitation programme started with trips round the block, on the lead, building up from just five minutes a *day* in week one to 60 minutes a day in week twelve. The early period of this curtailed activity was particularly trying because, as Gordon, the orthopaedic specialist, said to us, 'He'll feel fine, as though he could behave as normal.' In this way, a five-minute walk could take half an hour because Ollie developed a routine featuring any number of sit-down protests all the way round the block, i.e. every ten steps.

As the trips lengthened, and in contrast to our beginnings, it was *he* who came to pester *me* to take him out at night-time. He is a very strong dog – to complete the reversal of the early days, it was he who dragged me round the scary streets down to Carrow Road and back.

As the time neared when he received his clean bill of health, as his bone density returned, each day we went jogging together in parkland, still using the leash, just to get him moving a bit faster, and to warm his muscles. All this enforced proximity finalised our bond.

He actually came up to my office and wagged his tail. He will sit under my desk while I type now, and sometimes he will lick my bare feet, which can only mean they taste nice, like horse manure.

As the moment came closer for his life to return to normal, as I counted down to the official off-lead date, I found myself itching to slip the ring and let him go. Because there were two things I missed during the period of his confinement more than I would have imagined possible. One was watching him run. The other was walking with him, out in nature, seeing him free, and being free myself.

POSTSCRIPT TO THE FIRST EDITION

It would be remiss of me not to mention something that happened between the handing in of the original manuscript for *Walking Ollie*, the publication of the hardcover, and the reappearance of this book in paperback.

As Ollie 'normalised' (this will always remain a relative term, in his case), the something that happened was this: I became obsessed with the idea that what he really needed was a canine companion. I spent an ever increasing amount of time online looking at Lurcherlink and other lurcher rescue sites. Here I would read reports and study pictures of dogs that were, like Ollie at the outset, deserving cases, and worse. Occasionally I'd see one that I thought might make a good brother or sister for him, but I would step back from doing anything about it for the obvious reason: did I really want to go through all this again? The answer was, No.

So instead I took an obvious, lunatic, step sideways. At a certain point it occurred to me that to the best of my knowledge, we had never, on any of our walks, come across a pure Saluki, the breed to which I have always attributed the biggest part of Ollie's troubles. What would one be like, I wondered, in real life? I searched Saluki breeders. They were relatively few in number, but on one particular website I saw a gallery of dogs that were rather fine-looking and elegant. So I emailed the site asking if there were any plans for puppies. 'There may be,' came the reply.

Trezza and I drove down to see the breeder, who lives a couple of hours away from Norwich. She had six Salukis which were restricted to her kitchen as we arrived. As she opened the door to allow the pack into the lounge, all but one (the one who is reserved and shy, the Ollie) rushed at us immediately to say their Hellos with a normal measure of barking, licking and sniffing. After the excitement had died down, which took only a minute or two, they each settled onto their personal rugs and cushions and sat quietly observing us. The breeder was assessing us, too, to see if we might be fit persons to become potential new owners for her lineage, and I expected as much, from those early Vizsla days. What was surprising was that the dogs were examining us in the same way. Much as Yul Brynner does to Deborah Kerr in *The King and I*, we were given a thorough once-over. We were being weighed and measured. By dogs. I was much taken with this attitude, and with their general regal deportment. Most were 'feathered', that is with long frayed ears and a fringe running along the underside of the tail, but the future father was without these adornments; he was 'a smooth silver grizzle'. Grizzle is a term that describes the way his coat blended from one tone of silver to another. If he were a horse he would be that most beautiful of animals, a grey.

I arranged a second visit, during which we took Ollie down to see how he might get on with the father. I had one specific worry so far as proceeding further down this path was concerned – Ollie has become slightly selective, in a very specific sense: he will not run with some other hounds, those he thinks might be faster than him. We went out for a walk with the father, who had by now done his job – there was a litter on the way, and all was fine. He and Ollie got along well enough for me to dare to discuss matters of business, to ask how much one of the pups might cost. My guess was that they would come in steeper than a Vizsla. And so they did.

In my race-going circle we now have a new expression for a stake. 'A Monkey' (£500) is a phrase you hear shouted around a betting ring. If you ever see us at a course sticking 'a Saluki' on the nose, you'll know we feel a bit more confident than to mess around punting a mere five nicker on a horse.

At the outset of this book I have accused breeders of being mad, and yet, now the new boy is home, I consider 'a Saluki' a bargain for so delightful and engaging a creature. More surprising, my mate, a couldn't-care-less about-dogs race-going companion, concurred with this view when he came round to see the ludicrous new addition.

'What d'you reckon?' I asked, as the ten-week-old 'smooth silver grizzle' (he took after his father), named Dylan (after Bob) nuzzled into his lap.

'Money well spent,' came the reply.

He's a tough old boot, the couldn't-care-less about-dogs race-going companion, but I swear I saw a tear mist up in his eye.

The ten-week-old Dylan

Ollie's early opinion of his little brother appears to be altogether more circumspect. He is sitting up in my office, keeping as far out of the pup's way as possible: he regards him as a nuisance, with his blowing of milky bubbles and his cute-boy act. As I type out this post-script, Dylan has been with us only a matter of days. It is mid-November, outside the wind is howling and the rain is blowing in.

A few pages of helpful notes came in Dylan's starter pack, advice regarding exercise, development, health and so on. Here is his daily menu:

Diet:

Your puppy is on 5 meals per day (2 milk meals and 3 meat meals) as follows:

Between 7 and 8 am: A milk feed of goats milk and instant porridge with either a teaspoon of honey or a raw egg yolk. (I give about 3 milk meals per week with the egg yolk).

10 am: A meat feed of 50g of Wafcol Greyhound Racing Puppy and a heaped tablespoon of minced meat. The Wafcol needs to be soaked with boiled water and allowed to cool before adding the meat.

2 pm: Another meat feed of the same amounts as above.

6 pm: Another meat feed of the same amounts as above.

9-9:30 pm: A milk feed of goats milk and instant porridge with either an egg yolk or a teaspoon of honey.

You will find that each meal is eaten with gusto and woe betide you if you are late with the meal!

In the middle of the night I wake to comfort Dylan as he cries because he finds himself in unfamiliar new surroundings, away from the warmth of his siblings, albeit next to a radiator in a lovely new bed furnished with a hundred new throws that Trezza has brought home.

In the morning I cook up his nourishing breakfast, and a bowl for myself while I'm at it (in fact, I'm considering switching to his diet wholesale, he looks superb on it). As I move from fridge to pantry to cupboard to stove, and begin to stir the porridge, Dylan watches my every move, and yelps in anticipation of the great moment when his bowl goes down. I cannot help but compare his beginnings with Ollie's start in life.

It has been howling all night now, it has become a

gale, and the rain is sheeting down sideways. Dylan will not countenance going out in it, he shivers as I open the door, and he chooses to piss on an indoor pee-pad instead. It is the same time of year that Ollie was found in Thetford Forest, trying desperately, I imagine, to find anything to eat at all, and making do with whatever shelter he could find from weather like this. It makes me wonder, it does. When Dylan has cleaned up every last bit of breakfast, and Hoovered the floor roundabouts, I take Ollie a bowl of porridge upstairs too, and drop him in an extra spoonful of honey.

Stephen Foster is the author of the short story collection, *It Cracks Like Breaking Skin,* and the novel *Strides*, about love and trousers. *She Stood There Laughing*, his account of a season following Stoke City, was one of the bestselling sports books of 2004. He lives in Norwich with his partner and a lurcher called Ollie.

In case of difficulty in purchasing any Short Books
title through normal channels, please contact
BOOKPOST Tel: 01624 836000
Fax: 01624 837033
email: bookshop@enterprise.net
www.bookpost.co.uk
Please quote ref. 'Short Books'i